ATHLONE RENAISSANCE LIBRARY

Four Tudor Interludes

ATHLONE RENAISSANCE LIBRARY

MARGUERITE DE NAVARRE
Tales from the Heptaméron
edited by H. P. Clive

CALVIN
Three French Treatises
edited by Francis M. Higman

D'AUBIGNÉ
Les Tragiques (selections)
edited by I. D. McFarlane

JEAN DE LA TAILLE
Dramatic Works
edited by Kathleen M. Hall and C. N. Smith

ANTOINE DE MONTCHRESTIEN
Two Tragedies
edited by C. N. Smith

Tudor Verse Satire
edited by K. W. Gransden

Selected Writings of
FULKE GREVILLE
edited by Joan Rees

Four Tudor Interludes
edited by J. A. B. Somerset

Sonnets of
the English Renaissance
edited by J. W. Lever

Four
Tudor Interludes

edited by
J. A. B. SOMERSET

UNIVERSITY OF LONDON
THE ATHLONE PRESS
1974

Published by
THE ATHLONE PRESS
UNIVERSITY OF LONDON
at 4 Gower Street, London WC1

Distributed by
Tiptree Book Services Ltd
Tiptree, Essex

U.S.A. and Canada
Humanities Press Inc
New York

0 485 13602 3 *cloth*
0 485 12602 8 *paperback*

Printed in Great Britain by
WESTERN PRINTING SERVICES LTD
BRISTOL

PREFACE

The four pre-Shakespearian plays reprinted here will, it is hoped, provide some insight into the dramatic traditions behind the Elizabethan and Jacobean theatre. Choosing only four was not easy, since so many other early interludes remain relatively inaccessible to students and readers.

The Tudor theatre was very aware of conventions, and hence playwrights availed themselves of a common stock of situations, jokes, routines, and so on. In my introduction and commentary I have tried to suggest some of these and hence to indicate how the plays work upon audiences' expectations of the theatrical tradition.

My debt to previous investigators is partially reflected in the selected bibliography. For *Mankind*, Professor Mark Eccles's definitive edition (cited as E) has been very helpful, and I am grateful to him and to the Council of the Early English Text Society for permission to use extracts. I am also indebted to the Trustees of the British Museum, the Folger Shakespeare Library, the Bodleian Library, and the Pepysian Library, for permission to use the following as copy-texts:

Mankind. The Macro manuscript (Folger MS. V.a.354), fols. 122–34ᵣ.

A Play of Love. William Rastell, 1534 (folio). Pepysian Library.

An Enterlude Called Lusty Juventus. Abraham Vele, [1550?] (quarto). Bodleian Library.

An Enterlude Intituled Like Will to Like. John Allde, 1568 (quarto). Bodleian Library.

I would particularly like to thank the series' General Editor, Professor Geoffrey Bullough, for his tireless help and suggestions in editing these plays. For his encouragement and assistance in studying the early drama I am also deeply indebted to Dr Peter Davison, and for particular assistances I wish to thank Dr Gordon Greene.

I am grateful to the University of Western Ontario for assistance in purchasing materials and typing, and to the Director and fellows of the Shakespeare Institute, University of Birmingham, for

v

generously allowing me to use their collections. Finally, I have been greatly aided by the patience and advice of my wife, Felicity, to whom I dedicate this book.

London, Ontario   J.A.B.S.

vi

CONTENTS

NOTE ON THE TEXTS

I have preserved archaic forms of obsolete words, or where rhyme or metre dictate it. Added material, placed within square brackets, is present in two cases. First, stage directions have been added sparingly, where needed to indicate entrances and exits. Second, *lacunae* in the copy-text of *Lusty Juventus* have been remedied from the second quarto.

The copy-texts used are the earliest original versions as established (in the case of printed texts) by collation of the early editions. Some modern editions have also been examined. The relationship of the three undated quartos of *Lusty Juventus* has hitherto been uncertain, but Abraham Vele's quarto (c. 1550) appears to be the first edition. (The Malone Society reprint of the play reached me after I had completed my own textual work: J. M. Nosworthy, its editor, has come to the same conclusions in his thorough analysis.)

INTRODUCTION

The plays in this volume represent the remarkable range of drama in the late fifteenth and sixteenth centuries before the opening of permanent theatres. *A Play of Love* excepted, they might be termed 'morality plays', not only because of their moralizing aims but also their use of dramatized allegory. The characters mingle allegorical abstractions and social types (with a few non-allegorical figures such as the devil). I have called the plays 'interludes'—a common name reflected in the full titles of *Lusty Juventus* and *Like Will*. However, attempts to define the 'interlude' in terms of a particular type of play or performance are dangerous: it seems to have been used very loosely, meaning 'play'—a short drama written (most usually) for indoor performance.

Like the miracle cycles, the interludes have suffered from critical hostility. Hardin Craig writes that the genre

> retained the practice of introducing allegorical figures of virtues and vices on the stage, and this became its bane. These colourless abstractions became a *sine qua non* of the moral play and introduced themselves into other kinds of plays where they had no business to be. They were introduced without artistic propriety because they were expected to appear, so that they became mere symptoms of degenerate repetition.[1]

However the many surviving plays, the evidence of troupes and performances, and strenuous government efforts to control the stage all attest to its vitality and popularity, and make us hesitate to accept such a judgement. Like the miracle plays, the interludes were officially regarded as potentially dangerous. The crown had itself used the stage as a political and religious weapon under Thomas Cromwell's sponsorship, and it later attempted to control this impulse to propagandize.

Mankind (1470), *A Play of Love* (1528–33), *Lusty Juventus* (1550), and *Like Will to Like* (1568) might have constituted part of the repertoire of a troupe of professional players who travelled about and performed wherever an audience (and a chance of profit)

---

[1] *English Religious Drama* (Oxford, 1955), p. 378.

presented itself. These small groups of from four to eight actors can be traced in local records from all parts of England throughout the sixteenth century, in remarkable numbers. They were necessarily very versatile, having to double a wide variety of parts in many plays, and they were skilled at adapting plays to meet the various demands of 'playhouses' temporarily converted from other uses (town and guild halls, inns, churches, etc.).[2] The interludes make the best of their production style by employing an illusion which does not suggest realism but makes great use of symbols, comedy, and appeals to the audience through direct address.

As Professor Spivack has pointed out, a mankind figure should not require large forces of vices and virtues to cause his fall and repentance—intimate, single-handed persuasions could have more impact.[3] The hero's soul is our concern, and the allegorized drama of conflict undergoes a sea-change from the large outdoor morality plays of the fifteenth century to the much reduced sixteenth-century interludes. The versatility of the morality framework may help to explain its long continuance. Allegory is easily modified to suit various regions, social classes and interests, and it lends itself naturally to symbolism of action and costume (a pervasive sixteenth-century habit in dramatic and semi-dramatic entertainments).[4] As the three allegorical plays in this volume will testify, allegory was capable of great developments, from theological drama centred upon man (*Mankind*), to social satire centred upon the Vice (*Like Will*). The plays strive for relevance to the issues of the day, and present moral and ethical problems vividly through polarized clashes of argument and combat. The considerable influence they had on the Elizabethan and Jacobean drama bears witness to their versatility and vitality.[5]

Comic episodes for the vices occur in the earliest interludes, and comedy later develops markedly and is advertised on title-pages to buyers of plays. Perhaps, as some have argued, it is

[2] Glynne Wickham, *Early English Stages* (1959–63), ii (Part One), 153–206.

[3] *Shakespeare and the Allegory of Evil* (New York, 1958), p. 92.

[4] Wickham, ii, 206–44.

[5] E. T. Schell and J. D. Shuchter (eds.), *English Morality Plays and Moral Interludes* (New York, 1959), exemplify this view: 'the moralities were not replaced by a superior form of drama but rather absorbed into a different form' (p. vi).

'comic relief' from the sermons and arguments. But comedy is part of the vices' roles and thus affects our response to the debate: if we consider it as only relief we are implying that the plays are guilty of 'the dishonest trick of dragging in humour to amuse while pretending to condemn it'.[6] That the comedy has a moral purpose has also been suggested, but in terms that make the plays' humour virtually disappear. The hero's opening song in *Lusty Juventus* has been approached in this way:

The ditty of love longing...although its carolling birds in an 'herber green' and its dream-vision of a ladylove grace the English stage with the first thrills of the coming music, does not alter the point. The charm that suffuses it is inadvertent, and at odds with its purpose, which is to reveal the depraved state of the singer.[7]

Humour and charm become 'inadvertent' if we see comedy as a symbol of evil; hence critics who so argue stress that the comedy is scabrous, obscene, low buffoonery whose purpose is to horrify the audience. This mistakenly assumes that the plays are moral in *method* as well as purpose, constantly attempting to persuade us that vice is only to be condemned and virtue embraced.

In each moral interlude the hero undergoes a series of contrasting experiences and shows contrasting attitudes. The plays also display many varieties of humour, some of which do not horrify the hero or us. Mischief's comic impersonation of a quack doctor (*Mankind*, 430–48) delights us, while the later jokes accompanying the attempt to hang Mankind are horrifying. Conventional jokes are also common in the plays, such as the one (shared by our four plays) in which the vices invite others to kiss their buttocks. The moral purpose of each play is achieved when the hero, finally successful, sums up his experiences and his knowledge of the vices' evil: this follows the resolution of the conflict and the flight of the vices. Before this, vice and virtue have been at odds and the hero has been unable to choose properly between them. The hero vicariously represents us, and if we attend to his reactions we find he is sometimes strongly attracted to the vices, whose humour is a means of seduction (and hence a weapon in the conflict). It can attract us also. Comedy can suggest a joy in life and good times which only later turns out

---

[6] A. W. Pollard, 'Critical Essay', in C. M. Gayley, *Plays of our Forefathers* (New York, 1903), p. lv.
[7] Spivack, p. 218.

to be specious. For example, the vices in *Mankind* 'love well to make merry' (274), and after his seduction Mankind looks forward to a 'leman with a smattering face' (612). The vices' insistence upon good times is echoed by Falstaff when he is accused of being 'that reverend vice': 'if sack and sugar be a fault, God help the wicked! if to be old and merry be a sin, then many an old host that I know is damn'd; if to be fat be to be hated, then Pharaoh's lean kine are to be loved' (*I Henry IV*, II.iv.455). In the interludes, a striking feature is the remarkably frequent use of the vices' close rapport with the audience in order to persuade us directly to sympathize with them. Titivillus promises us 'a good sport' (*Mankind*, 587), No-lover-nor-loved assumes (rightly) that we are on his side (*Love*, 415). Juventus wants us to 'game' (*Juventus*, 57), and Nichol makes us laugh at the discomfiture of auditors such as 'Joan with the long snout' (*Like Will*, 227). We see, then, that the vices are speciously alluring and hence we can understand how the hero might be tempted to yield, while at other times the evil and grotesque nature of the vices is predominant. They are damnable, but damned funny, while on the other hand the morally upright virtues usually seem very strait-laced and dull. Similarly, Falstaff shows his impossibility as a counsellor to a king, while his humanity and warmth make us wish that his banishment were not inevitable. While not approaching Shakespeare's subtlety of characterization, the writers of vice comedy seem to share his aim of polarizing a conflict and then forcing a resolution through events.

II

From among the vices there emerged a major character who was to remain prominent in the memories of the Elizabethans as the epitome of the moral interludes—'the Vice'. He appears in this volume in *Love* and *Like Will*—the former marks his first recorded appearance. The Vice, generally identified with evil, mischief, or nihilism, was not normally required to be doubled. Title-pages reflect his growing eminence (e.g., *A New Enterlude of Vice Containing the History of Horestes*) and the appearances of 'the Vice' in twenty extant plays suggest that the character became a conventional part of the popular drama. 'The Vice' also is found in other sources which often suggest a kinship with the Elizabethan clown. At Bungay in 1566, for example, a payment is recorded 'to Kelsaye, the vice, for his pastyme before the plaie, and after the plaie, both daies ij^s'.[8]

The interludes show in many other ways that they are popular theatre—highly conventional works which repeat well-known comic and other motifs. Heywood's borrowing from this tradition to create a 'Vice' who shares many traits with his fellows is evidence that by 1525 a recognizable body of comic devices existed. While various pieces of comic business may have originally had some symbolic or homiletic function, they apparently came to be elaborated for their humour alone. As humour they often depend upon the audience's prior expectations, becoming all the more humorous because they are repeated, stock, 'old turkeys'. A few of the comic routines in *Like Will*, together with analogies and antecedents, will illustrate this dependence upon conventional humour. Nichol first recounts his 'whole education' (52)—a comic account of his apprenticeship in the Devil's tailoring shop. This vice-pedigree, or account of previous off-stage actions, is common: the vices in *Mankind* recount their experiences as horse-thieves (614 ff.), and No-lover-nor-loved entertains us with his past history as a mock lover (*Love*, 420 ff.). In *The Trial of Treasure* (1567) occurs a remarkable comic pedigree from Inclination, who begins,

> I can remember since Noe's ship
> Was made, and builded on Salisbury plain;
> The same year the weathercock of Paul's caught the pip
> So that Bow-bell was like much woe to sustain.
> I can remember, I am so old,
> Since Paradise gates were watched by night
> And when that Vulcanus was made a cuckold...[9]

This fustian is matched by the first introduction of Idleness in *The Marriage of Wit and Wisdom* (1579):

> my mother had ii whelpes at one litter
> both borne in lent
> so we ware both put into a Musselbote
> & came saling in a sowes yeare ouer sea
> into kent[10]

Another common routine uses legal situations. Nichol assumes a judge's role and defends his 'powers' in a petulant comic quarrel

---

[8] E. K. Chambers, *The Medieval Stage* (Oxford, 1903), ii, 343.
[9] Quoted in Dodsley, *A Select Collection of Old English Plays*, ed. W. Carew Hazlitt (1874–6), iii, 267.
[10] Malone Society Reprints (Oxford, 1971), 197.

(*Like Will*, 319 ff.), paralleling Mischief's mock court (*Mankind*, 655 ff.) and the comic judgeship of No-lover-nor-loved (*Love*, 805 ff.). Linguistic jokes, making fun of Latin or the dialect of particular characters, are common to *Mankind*, *Like Will*, and many other plays, and show that Shakespeare's Holofernes in *Love's Labour's Lost* has many ancestors. Closely akin to comic language are the frequent proverbs. My notes draw on M. P. Tilley's *The Proverbs of England in the Sixteenth and Seventeenth Centuries* (1950) to point out direct parallels and possible analogies. Proverbs (e.g., 'a stitch in time saves nine') today often pass unnoticed, but Tudor playgoers and readers were addicted to them and to adages, epigrams, aphorisms, and similar pithy sayings. Men took pride in the range of proverb lore they had mastered, perhaps keeping 'tables' (as does Hamlet) to record new acquisitions. A remarkable number of proverb collections followed the fashion set by Heywood's *A Dialogue Containing the Number in Effect of all the Proverbs in the English Tongue* (1546)—a book which endeared Heywood to his age far more than his plays.

III

Mankind has generally been attacked by critics. J. Q. Adams thought the play to be a reworked version in which serious elements had been eliminated in favour of buffoonery (though there is no manuscript evidence to support such a theory). Tucker Brooke similarly saw the play as 'diverted to the production of buffoonery', while in Smart's view the play contains little theology and is 'a sham morality, with a slight morality framework...whose chief business is to entertain'. A. W. Pollard saw the play as a burlesque, because the audience is persuaded to side with the vices, and Hardin Craig finds a reason for this in the play's performance by a travelling troupe: hence it was badly abridged and 'carried on the road for one does not know how long by a low-class company of strolling players, whose appeal was to the uneducated and the vulgar...yokels and the toughs of small towns'.[11] In many of these criticisms one finds

[11] J. Q. Adams (ed.), *Chief Pre-Shakespearian Dramas* (Boston, 1926), p. 304; C. F. Tucker Brooke, *The Tudor Drama* (Boston, 1911), p. 63; W. K. Smart, 'Some Notes on *Mankind*', *Modern Philology*, xiv (1916), 118, A. W. Pollard (ed.), *English Morality Plays and Moral Interludes*, 8th edn (Oxford, 1927), pp. lv–lvi; Craig, pp. 350–1.

the implied wish that *Mankind* were longer, more serious, more theological—in short, more like *The Castle of Perseverance*. It is however possible to see serious moral aspects in *Mankind*, as the interlude presents in its short compass a consistent theological message about man's nature. Equally, one can see the comic antics as lively, high-spirited, and functional.

Mercy was one of the four daughters of God (Psalm 85:10) whose debate before God was a common medieval theme. Justice, Truth, and Equity (Righteousness) are mentioned (845–61), but Mercy alone appears here, characterized as a friar.[12] His role is a dual one: at times he abstractly represents his quality, mercy, and at others he saves from sin more humanly and concretely. His opening, prayerful lesson establishes a general frame of reference by setting sinfulness against the mercy shown in Christ's passion and death, before the vices enter with their taunts. Mercy has been found wanting by some critics, and indeed this dissatisfaction often seems to lie at the bottom of adverse criticisms of *Mankind*. That Mercy is far outnumbered by vices surely matters less than his final success against great odds. But Mercy has been accused of 'schoolboy heroics', and Pollard thought that the author deliberately makes fun of Mercy by having him speak 'English Latin' (aureate diction), unintelligible to audiences.[13] Leaving aside such hypotheses as to what earlier audiences could understand, we note that it is the vices' japes and jeers which make us sharply aware of Mercy's speech-style. Mischief, New Guise, Naught, and Nowadays taunt Mercy because of his logic and Latinisms, and they injure his dignity by tripping him up. We need not agree that his ornate fustian makes him merely ridiculous, though we may feel that the vices score a point from time to time (for example, in asking him to construe nonsense, 122–39). Mercy's style can be defended on grounds of decorum since his Latinisms give him dignity, which is furthered by his slow, measured verse and intricate stanzaic forms of (usually) four and eight lines, often rhyme-linked. Also, his use of dignified Scriptural quotations and Latin aphorisms suggests learning. Finally, the dignity of Mercy's speeches is as *austere* as are his other-worldly homiletics, so his style characterizes his way of life.

[12] Sister Phillipa Coogan, *An Interpretation of the Moral Play, 'Mankind'* (Washington, D.C., 1947), pp. 2, 5.
[13] *English Miracle Plays*, p. lvi.

7

The fight between Mercy and the vices establishes dramatic contrast and a homiletic focus on sins of the flesh,[14] and after this Mankind enters the play: representing us, he must choose between the alternatives. Mankind shares Mercy's style and vocabulary here, suggesting his innocent holiness. He is full of precepts about his human nature and fearful that his body— 'that stinking dunghill'—will cause his soul to fall. It is probably mistaken to view Mankind here as a sinner: he recoils in terror from that possibility and rather seems untried by life. His notice of the audience as 'this whole congregation' universalizes his speeches—the problem of sin is a general problem. Mankind, like ourselves, has a second problem: he sees himself as inevitably 'unsteadfast in living' and needing 'supportation' (212–14). Mercy admits that Mankind may well fall rather than persevere and can only advise him to soldier on to the best of his abilities, as did Job (280–90). Even as Mercy advises, however, the vices indicate through their off-stage jeers their confidence that Mankind will be theirs. In the face of this, Mercy makes what seems an unmotivated exit: realizing that the vices 'will be here right soon, if I out depart' (257), he yet leaves Mankind to face them alone. The doctrinal point is clear, however—the Christian must face life on his own, trusting in what Milton's Adam called 'single virtue'—and Mercy's exit both emphasizes this and makes Mankind more human, because more exposed.

Before tracing the action further, a look at the vices will show how attention to man's fleshly weaknesses is also obtained through them. Rather than allegorically standing for specific sins, New Guise, Naught, and Nowadays represent good-for-nothing social types who taken together are the 'way of the world'. Mischief, the fourth of the group, may partly allegorize suicide (cf. 894), but he is also a local tough, and in sum the four represent Mankind's earthly destiny if he yields to sin. Attention to sins of the flesh is constantly maintained through the vices' language, jokes, and concern for their own all-important creature comforts. Mercy is cursed for interrupting sleeping and eating (98–100) and later we witness a feast (630–50). Mischief tells there how his flight from prison was delayed by lechery and gluttony. Other bodily pleasures are dancing (in which Mercy will not join) and the game of football. The most cutting jibes the vices make are

[14] Siegfried Wenzel, *Acedia: The Sin of Sloth* (Chapel Hill, N.C., 1967), pp. 150–5.

8

those inviting Mercy to console his body: 'Your pottage shall be forcold, sir; when will ye go dine' (269); 'My prepotent father, when ye sup, sup out your mess' (777). Perhaps these body-worshipping vices can think of no other mode of existence. The scatological jokes and the dirty song they sing likewise allude to lechery, gluttony, and the health of the bowels. While we laugh we are being reminded of 'that stinking dunghill' the body. Stylistically the vices' speeches contrast strikingly with those of Mercy, as the conscious artistry of the playwright has fitted them with appropriately racy doggerel, tumbling metres, tail rhymes, and rhymes which are often inexact.

As Eccles notes, New Guise, Naught, and Nowadays are good-for-nothing, not even for seduction,[15] as their frontal assault earns them only a beating with the symbol of Mankind's labour, his spade. Mankind can defend himself against overt evils—he is well intentioned and not an easy victim. When the vices return to the empty stage, they attempt to ingratiate themselves with us (413–608) using the same methods formerly employed on the hero. We are invited to sympathize and assist with their future schemes. Before Titivillus appears the vices collect entrance money from the audience in a unique manner (that 'ye pay all alike' shows it is really admission-money). This allows the vices a chance to mingle humorously with the audience and improvise dialogue for 'a fair while' (473). We are being disarmed through comedy, and giving money symbolizes our agreement that Titivillus is worth paying to see. He maintains that he is a fine fellow and our special friend, whose efforts deserve sympathy. Lines such as 'And ever ye did, for me keep now your silence;/Not a word, I charge you, pain of forty pence' (590–1), suggest that we could warn Mankind, but we do not. We enjoy a 'good sport' instead, performed by a villain who reminds us of vaudeville in his close rapport with us, playing upon dramatic illusion. As well as these direct appeals, there is a great deal else to amuse us in the vices, such as Mischief's quack doctoring (a folk drama motif) and the tricking of Titivillus out of the collection-money. This humour disarms us, so we are later rudely awakened when the dangerous aspects of vice are emphasized—for example, when Titivillus sends his subordinates off to steal. The hero later undergoes a similar progression of responses, being at first put off guard and only later seeing whereto his life in sin is leading him.

[15] *The Macro Plays*, p. xliii.

9

Farce-trickery enters the interlude with the comic ploy of hiding the board in the ground, but there is more to Mankind's downfall than that. Rather than being just a hapless victim of the sly devil's tricks and the suggestions made to him while sleeping, Mankind is unsteadfast and slothful and hence he contributes to his fall. When labour becomes difficult it is quickly abandoned. Pathetically eager to believe that 'A short prayer thirleth Heaven', Mankind shows his lapse into sloth by arising from prayer (mortification of the flesh) to look after his body's needs by defecating in the yard. The colic and stone worry him more than his soul. (This episode also recalls the 'Christmas song'.) His sleep upon returning symbolizes sloth (cf. Hance's sleep in *Like Will*) and in sleep he is tricked into idolizing bodily pleasures because his weakness and sin make him unable to withstand Titivillus. Upon awakening, Mankind's second thought concerns lechery.

Returning to the vices (whom he earlier abhorred) Mankind follows his sinful way with open eyes. His fall is not yet complete and occurs in several stages. When he first greets the vices his first reactions are those of a wide-eyed spectator (613–60) in contrast to the utter depravity the vices reveal through their stories and actions (murder, robbing 'a church here beside' (635), rape of a gaoler's wife, etc.). Dramatic symbols make clear Mankind's progress in evil. His long side-gown is twice shortened, becoming the 'new guise' (short coats were forbidden to those under the rank of gentleman in sumptuary laws of 1463 and 1482).[16] The mock court successively enrols Mankind for various sins (chiefly gluttony, lechery, and wrath). Mankind's speech-style degenerates—he comes to sound more and more like the vices as well as looking and acting like them. Like Marlowe's Faustus, Mankind does not escape morality and become free; he merely exchanges masters.

Professor Coogan has suggested that there is confusion in the action between 732–804, especially in the treatment of Mercy.[17] We may see the confusion as being within Mankind, and Mercy's two appearances as indicating stages of Mankind's sinfulness. The hero begins by believing Mercy dead (666) and yet greets him without alarm (732), ignoring his persuasions and delaying a meeting until 'to-morn or the next day'. This encounter shows

---

[16] Smart, pp. 112–13.   [17] *An Interpretation*, p. 94.

the numbing effects of sin—Mankind thinks he can have fun now and temporize with God. Later, when he is told that Mercy still seeks him everywhere (805) this comfortable numbness deserts Mankind and he descends to the last stage—despair, the ultimate and unpardonable sin.

Writing about *Everyman*, A. C. Cawley alludes to 'what Coleridge might have called the "prudential calculus" of the medieval moral plays'[18]—whereby the plays show that man can sin today and repent tomorrow because repentance is always open to the sinner. *Mankind* is certainly not guilty of this 'calculus', although the hero is. The stages of sin are carefully delineated and Mercy explicitly rules out sinning in hope of repentance. Mankind's greatest danger is this 'calculus' which finally leads to attempted suicide—a close brush with death and Hell.

Mercy's final actions and teachings give the play its theological and dramatic coherence. He twice attempts to save Mankind (thus emphasizing his love for him). Between these attempts, Mercy speaks of the twin themes we have been following: 'Mankind is so flexible' (746), 'so wanton and so frail' (761). It is his final task to bring Mankind to a proper realization of these weaknesses. Mercy finally frightens the vices away (symbolically scaring sinfulness out of Mankind) but only after sin has run its full course to despair. As Mankind lies on the stage, Mercy first discusses Mankind's flexibility and convinces the hero that 'prudential calculus' will not work. Mankind's despair has led to obstinacy—a conviction that mercy is impossible—and in overcoming this Mercy proclaims the need for repentance. The two proverbs (840, 887) stress that Mankind's course has been ultimately for his good since he has added experiential knowledge of sin to his earlier innocent horror of it. It will be easier to avoid next time. Finally Mercy turns to the theme of man's fleshliness, explaining the action in terms of the traditional Seven Deadly Sins (888–94). The ne'er-do-wells are, appropriately, seen as 'worldly', and 'the Flesh' is assigned to Mankind himself, as the weakness of the individual's bodily nature, which craves attention and care at the expense of his soul. As Mercy says, 'Your body is your enemy; let him not have his will' (902).

Mercy is finally successful, and so is the play—it presents specific teaching in an ordered way through the resources of the theatre. Attempts to find a source for *Mankind* have failed, possibly

18 *Everyman*, ed. A. C. Cawley (Manchester, 1961), p. v.

because having begun with a pre-existent dramatic form and an idea of his theme, the playwright availed himself fully of the resources of theology. *Mankind* may be a Lenten play as Coogan suggests, since it is concerned with penance and other such observances.[19] However these themes have a wider application and the play would have been appropriate at any time, since man's frail human nature is always pertinent to a concern for salvation.

IV

John Heywood's *Play of Love* exemplifies new directions in the interlude arising from the humanist theatre at the Tudor court. Heywood and others dispensed with moral allegory and searched for models in other dramatic traditions more in keeping with the humanists' cosmopolitan interests in European literature and classical revival. The interlude offered these men the adaptability referred to earlier—their plays take up such interests as education, science, geography and exploration, and the proper rule of a kingdom, and are secular plays of discussion, not action.

Heywood's *Love* depends upon French models, as has long been recognized,[20] for at the time of composition France was much in vogue on account of Wolsey who (in 1529) 'does not wish anything to be said here which is not French in deed and in word'.[21] A view of Heywood which saw his dramatic practice as opportunistic would be unjust, however, since there are links between his entertaining little plays and those of the interluders. His purposes are similar to those of dramatists inculcating morality through allegory, and he is more than the 'mad merry Heywood' of tradition. He shares a serious concern with ideas and the intellectual agility of debate, but his debates differ from the moral allegories which end by totally rejecting one set of opponents, and their arguments. In *Love*, reconciliation of seemingly impossible opposites occurs, in the tradition of Lucianic dialogues. Henry Medwall's *Fulgens and Lucrece* (c. 1495) is comparable—it presents debaters representing nobility of birth and worth, and a clear-

---

[19] *An Interpretation*, pp. 20–5.
[20] Ian Maxwell, *French Farce and John Heywood* (Melbourne, 1946), *passim*.
[21] Quoted from a letter by the French Ambassador in 1529, by Sidney Thomas, 'Wolsey and French Farces', *TLS*, 7 December 1935, p. 838.

cut decision between them is impossible, as everyone agrees by the end of the play. While the morality framework would be inappropriate for these debate plays, the debates are concerned with ideas and situations of interest to their audiences. Heywood is an entertainer, but we may see him as writing for a theatre of ideas and propagating the ideas of the Sir Thomas More circle with which he was associated.[22]

Heywood's concern with pleasure and pain in love is reflected in the contrasts between the two pairs of disputants. The characters professing pleasure in love are somewhat individualized: the Vice, No-lover-nor-loved, a merry nihilist, is pitted against a self-satisfied and pompous opponent, Lover-loved, whose habit of uttering moral aphorisms draws attention to himself. In addition, Lover-loved's condescension to others depicts him as a fitting target of the Vice's sallies and 'squib' joke. Lover-loved must experience the pangs of another state of love, rather than just understand how others feel. On the other side, Lover-not-loved and Loved-not-loving are not individualized at all: each is merely the reverse of the other, and they are similarly hopeless victims.

The play's action suggests that pleasure consists in the (perhaps temporary) absence of pain in love, the latter being the more usual state of affairs. More attention is devoted to pain, as the 'pained' characters argue their cases twice before any development of the case for pleasure. Pain can speedily succeed pleasure, as Lover-loved's grief over the news of the supposed death of his mistress demonstrates (1332): on the other hand, pain in love seems a settled and hopeless state.

The niceties of arguments advanced, refuted, developed, and proved doubtless greatly interested audiences who were professionally concerned with diplomacy, the law, and the court. The first phase, in rhyme-royal, introduces us to the hopeless pain of Lover-not-loved—he is apparently lost in his pangs, and ignores the audience for some time. Pain meets pain when Loved-not-loving enters and each denies the case of the other (suggesting that both are partly wrong). Each character develops two arguments. Loved-not-loving establishes that her case is painful (to

---

[22] John Heywood's wife, Elizabeth Rastell, was Sir Thomas More's niece. As a singer and player of the virginals, Heywood was employed at the courts of Henry VIII and Mary. The best biographical accounts are in Bolwell and Johnson (cf. Bibliography).

115), thereby disproving Lover-not-loved; secondly she argues the intensity of her pain, saying that being disagreeably loved is more intolerable because the pain is incessant (to 160). Similarly, Lover-not-loved begins with a disproof, showing how a short pain can be worse than a long one (to 194), and then he goes on to argue the severity of his sharp pains (to 230). While the result is inconclusive, it is hinted that agreement probably lies somewhere between the extreme positions of the disputants, who can agree only that their cases are hopeless.

Pleasure is introduced by Lover-loved's truism concerning appearance and reality which has little immediate relationship to love. It is appropriate to the character in view of the Vice's later trick, which shows pleasure in love to be dependent upon appearances. The Vice's uncivil deflation of Lover-loved causes such antagonism that their need for an arbiter is apparent, and the acrimony between them ironically contrasts with their supposed state of pleasure. When Lover-loved goes to seek an umpire the play's first phase (simple oppositions of pain and pleasure) ends. The pairs of disputants thus far seem irreconcilable.

The process of the play is educative: the characters all begin by supposing themselves experts in all questions of love, but they come to learn wider views. The Vice's refusal to learn—'May I not think my pleasure more than his?' (1553)—emphasizes this. Although the characters are not brought together for some time, and although the arguments imply great differences in viewpoints, there are hints of reconciliation from the beginning since the characters are constantly anticipating or echoing each others' statements. To take only a few examples, Lover-not-loved and Lover-loved agree that all values are summed up in the loved one and that love is all-powerful (cf. 20 and 267). Lover-not-loved's admission that he presses his suit at all times (48) comically anticipates the Vice's disregard—'In time not too timely—such time as I could' (509), and the woes he mentions are echoed in the Vice's experiences. The Vice, it seems, has the least to learn about love and the least direct experience of it, and he has an important part to play in resolving the arguments. Perhaps to enhance his role the style changes to rhyming couplets when he enters, and certainly his appearance brings energy to the play.

The Vice asserts his knowledge of love in his catalogue of the types of women (350–64) and his story, which is more than a 'pastance', although its fabliau-like humour enlivens the play greatly. It presents a view of physical love and parodies the attitudes of all four of the play's disputants. The Vice assumes the guise of a lover not loved whose woeful 'hopes and dread' (549) parallel Lover-not-loved (219–20). Playing the lover loved, the Vice parodies sweetly sentimental 'lovebirds' (580–605), echoing Lover-loved: all the while the Vice believes he is a man loved not loving. When he disappears (attempting to end the affair) the tables are turned. Fearing his mistress's grief as a lover not loved (like Lover-loved's grief that his lady has been burnt), the Vice returns to find himself mocked—his mistress, like himself, has been no lover nor loved. This parody contrasts with the other characters' seriousness, pointing out, as does Touchstone in *As You Like It*, that love is laughable rather than calamitous. The ease with which guises are switched in the tale suggests that there is some feigning in all love and refutes Lover-loved's aphorism, 'love his appearance dissembleth in no wise' (261), especially since the shrewd Vice was fooled into thinking 'she loved me perfectly' (600). Other common assumptions are mocked, such as the idea that unrequited lovers always die.

Upon their return the Vice arranges the characters into four combinations having common factors, since the pairings which first met and debated have nothing in common. Those who are lovers (788) and those who are not (790) are contrasted by their mistresses' attitudes. Happiness or unhappiness can stem from others. Pain or pleasure can be self-inflicted, as is shown by the pairings of those not loved (789) and those who are loved (791), wherein the contrast arises between subjectively loving or not loving. As the argument will show, each sufferer wishes for pleasure, and the happy assume that their state of mind is permanent.

The dispute is rejoined over the possibility of subjective changes of attitude. While she could never become a lover, Loved-not-loving paradoxically asks why Lover-not-loved does not 'will love to refrain' (914). Over reason and the affections, disagreement erupts among the judges: Lover-loved naturally sees the force of love as beyond the will, while the Vice agrees with Loved-not-loving that one can at least stop loving where it is hopeless. Agreement is finally reached that 'will will not be/ Forced in love' (969), so a solution is impossible and the pains of love continue. There are ample explanations of the intensity of these pains (in terms recalling Petrarchanism) and the Vice's sardonic jokes make fun of pain by treating it as physical, not emotional (1024 ff.). (One wonders how much distress is actually present, especially when the suffering souls soon apparently forget their pangs and act as judges of pleasure.) Imaginative transference of roles ends matters (just as it caused the humour of the Vice's story). Lover-not-loved sees the dilemma: he cannot say that he would prefer another kind of pain, being a man loved, but not loving (1038 ff.).

The happy characters, in their turn, move quickly to defining pleasure as opposed to contentation (contentment). Both disputants attempt to defend impossible dialectical arguments, but have better luck with ones which are more restrained. First, Lover-loved confuses voluntary and involuntary contentation, trying to argue that all contentation is involuntary (1120–40). His second and better argument is that pleasure is above contentation. The Vice weakly tries to prove pleasure and love to be incompatible (1183 ff.) in a tirade which seeks to convince by quantity rather than quality of argument. His summation of the pains of a lover more aptly describes Lover-not-loved than his opponent, and he ends in nonsense concerning 'black jaundice' (1222). Neither character can totally deny validity to his opponent, so common ground is approached, beginning with agreement that there can be pleasure in love (1250). Over the question of pain, Lover-loved totally denies that he could suffer it and this self-satisfaction makes him a ready target for the Vice's trick. This second story from No-lover-nor-loved (really an argument by example) plunges Lover-loved into the temporary woes of being a lover not loved, and the ridiculous figure he cuts on stage as well as the jests directed at him by the Vice (1340–52) suitably repay his presumption. Parallels between the two stories (in both, for example, the Vice observes a woman through a window) perhaps suggest how the Vice so readily concocts the second tale. Upon his return, Lover-loved tries to evade his evident 'dismaying' but eventually must agree that love can be painful. Paradoxically, this strengthens the case Lover-loved had begun to make earlier (1250), and to which he returns by asking not who enjoys more pleasure, but how the extreme emotions of pleasure and pain (in love) may be compared with the evenness of contentation (1420 ff.). From here a new synthesis is reached in which the Vice's contentation becomes a standard to set against pain or pleasure.

The solution matters less than the course of the debate and what it has shown about love—that pleasure in love is impermanent, while pain remains. Happiness cannot be wished since 'will will not be forced by love' (the type-names, which identify characters and attitudes, strengthen this idea). Unable to reform, the characters cannot expect their opposites to change, so each character is the prisoner of himself and another—we have a growing sense that there are not four characters involved in this play, but seven, because the three characters involved with love continuously refer to their offstage partners. The exception is the contented Vice, whose lover is fictional (and, like him, no lover nor loved). His state provides the norm, and against this pleasure and pain in love have come to be seen as closely allied (if not actually the same emotion) and dependent ultimately upon others. The Vice has changed only in so far that he now will admit some value in love, although his agreement is extremely limited.

Be it pleasurable or painful (or laughable) human love is imperfect and so it completes the treatment of love in the play to refer to divine love as a higher harmony. Stylistically, the coming of agreement has been accompanied by a return to rhyme-royal (1501 ff.). The harmony of the play's ending is contentation (or agreement), above which is true pleasure in divine love, with which the play's Christmas audience could heartily concur.

V

R. Wever (*Lusty Juventus*) and Ulpian Fulwell (*Like Will to Like*) were probably both clergymen,[23] and their plays are late moral interludes concerned with religious polemic and social satire. The tumbling irregular metres, endstoppage, and rhyme which C. S. Lewis labelled 'drab' prevent our calling either playwright a good poet, but one notices some attempts at metrical variation. Songs punctuate the action and provide contrast, both with other songs and with the speech styles. As in *Mankind*, an attempt is made in both plays to suit diction and metre to

[23] The few conjectures about R. Wever are in *Lusty Juventus*, ed. J. M. Nosworthy, Malone Society Reprints (Oxford, 1971), p. xxii. More is known about Ulpian Fulwell, because of a controversy over another of his books, *Ars Adulandi* (1576). He was rector of Naunton, Glos., from 1570 to 1586. (Cf. Bibliography for Irving Ribner's two articles.)

character, and this heightens the contrast between the dignity of the virtues and unregeneracy of the vices. While the verse may be hard for some to appreciate, reciting it aloud will show that there is more variation in it than meets the eye.

The contrasting structures of *Lusty Juventus* and *Like Will* are evidence of experimentation in diverse ways of writing plays for a small company. In *Mankind*, interaction of characters is easy since the play has only seven parts for six actors, but when the number of parts is enlarged through doubling, coherence is not always easily maintainable. *Lusty Juventus* is akin to *Mankind* in that, most of the time, it coheres about the mankind hero. Its doubling works for four actors:

1 – Juventus	3 – Good Counsel
	Fellowship
2 – Prologue	4 – Knowledge
Satan	Hypocrisy
Abominable Living	God's Merciful Promises

As Juventus meets all the characters except Satan, his part cannot be doubled and has the greatest continuity. In contrast, *Like Will* is Vice-centred, as its title-page doubling chart indicates (see p. 128), and it does not have a central hero. Nichol Newfangle, the Vice, meets virtually everyone, whereas the chief virtue, Virtuous Life, appears only twice in isolated episodes and does nothing to tie the play together structurally. The Vice soliloquizes a great deal, filling the times while other actors change roles (e.g., 565–600), commenting to us about the various characters he meets and generally becoming very friendly with us.

Both plays introduce the Devil, but as little more than an ugly buffoon with little part in the action. The vices link our world and Hell; being speciously attractive they are able to move about in the world. The Devil provides comedy which arises from visual grotesquerie (masks, fireworks, etc.), and from the somewhat standoffish relationship between father-devil and son-vice. Mockery and misunderstandings abound, revealing the true nature of the evil characters, but the Devil is either wrong-headed or irrelevant to the action. In *Lusty Juventus* he is over-pessimistic (375–445) and finally he has to leave the engineering of a plot to Hypocrisy because he doesn't really know the world's ways. In *Like Will*, Nichol reproves Lucifer for giving him commands which are outdated—'Tush, tush, that is already brought to pass' (111), and the hapless Devil, instead of planning the downfall of the world, finds himself merely describing its present nature—a splendid opportunity for the dramatist's social and religious satire (cf. Ben Jonson's *The Devil is an Ass*, I. i). Like Milton's Satan, these devils recognize the goodness in the world but disapprove of it and wish to pervert it to evil; however, they are surprised to find the job already well under way.

Both plays are ardently Protestant and pessimistic about mankind—the pessimism may well suggest Calvinism.[24] In *Lusty Juventus* to live well means doing what is 'appointed in the Scripture' (81) according to Protestant dictates, chiefly justification by faith (220), and to depend upon God's word in Scripture to the total exclusion of ignorant tradition (247–8). When Juventus meets Hypocrisy, the Vice mocks his great learning, re-establishes a reverence for tradition, and jeers him away from his Protestant virtues (582–665). Hypocrisy's Catholic arguments are composed of sarcasm and threats, not logic, and the positive claims for Catholicism are not allowed to develop (see the notes). The last phase of the play carries forward the Protestant polemic. Good Counsel's lament over Juventus becomes generalized (901–35), so questions such as 'who readeth the Scripture to the intent to follow it?' (918) are asked of us. Juventus is finally saved according to the Protestant doctrine of salvation through the merits of Christ (1066).

The play teaches that the child is father of the man, so careful training must be given to young people (15–17, 347–8). Juventus is a 'young man', desirous to learn from and follow his mentors, and pathetically eager for friends and comradeship. He enters looking for a group of friends, admitting that 'To be alone is not my appety' (61). His friendship shifts to his virtuous colleagues, whom he promises never to forsake, and then to Hypocrisy and his fellows (who masquerade as Friendship and Fellowship). Hypocrisy claims old acquaintance with Juventus (561–6) and insinuates that Juventus will be 'out of the winning' (584) and 'lose all your friends' goodwill' (630) unless he forsakes virtue. These arguments are hard to resist and Juventus feels caught between companions. Whom will he follow? When he says he 'must needs go' to the sermon (661), the sense of duty contrasts with his earlier *desire* to go, and he is diverted by the promise of

[24] David Bevington, *From 'Mankind' to Marlowe* (Cambridge, Mass., 1962), p. 152.

pleasure at breakfast and 'merry company' (705). The long argument over who is Juventus's greatest friend among the three vices (825–78) also makes him feel befriended.

One might well ask, what chance has such a young man to remain steadfastly virtuous? Certainly Knowledge has little faith in Juventus. He sees his virtue as 'profession', and questions if Juventus will 'live according' (311–12). Juventus's course leaves one pessimistic. The title-page announces that youth is naturally prone to vice but possibly grace and good counsel can bring him to virtue; and it is as naturally vicious (or, unregenerate and ignorant) that Juventus enters. When converted from his blind deception, his truculence allows the dramatist to propound a great deal of doctrine, as does Juventus's habit of repeating things which he learns (e.g., 250–60). The hero then reflects the attitudes of his companions and seems to surpass their piety. Later (860 ff.), Juventus is similarly more wrathful and argumentative than the other vices. His moral and emotional shifts are violent. Since he has been won from his lusts to virtue, thence to vice, and finally to virtue again, one wonders finally about the quality of this repentance. Will it last?

One also wonders from what the final repentance proceeds, and if it is free from all taint of the 'prudential calculus' mentioned earlier. When Juventus encounters Good Counsel he argues heatedly with him, apparently feeling no guilt and repeating a 'smart aleck' remark suggested by Hypocrisy (963). Only after a lengthy reproof by Good Counsel, during which he is told that those who sin after receiving the truth are irrevocably damned, does Juventus repent, feeling despairingly that 'it is too late' (1012). Then, rather amazingly, Good Counsel cheerfully turns to discussing God's mercy, and God's Promises later points out that Juventus has misunderstood the Pauline doctrine of inevitable damnation (1055–6). Really, it seems that Good Counsel misuses the doctrine to *induce* despair and repentance—which in turn lead to forgiveness through faith. Thus 'prudential calculus' operates, since the danger of despair and death (so immediate in *Mankind*) is not present here. The final lengthy moralization by the regenerate Juventus adds little; it rather recounts than sums up his experiences in the action and gives little sense of the relief of being spared. As Nosworthy says (p. xxiii), the interlude is notable more for its piety than for its poetry—and, we might add, more for its doctrine than for its drama.

VI

By its presentation of social groups, *Like Will to Like* impresses on us that social and moral evil are allied, the crimes being similar to those reprehended by Puritan moralists such as Philip Stubbes. The decay of vice promised (Prologue, 18) turns out to be its defeat and punishment in this world, not its final damnation. As the final prayer makes clear, moral well-being in the state follows upon clarity and fairness of the law and the government. Severity the Judge is the sole figure of retribution (except Nichol Newfangle), and his justice is concerned with hanging—an earthly punishment. No repentance is possible for the evil-doers of the play to alleviate their punishment. Although Cutbert Cutpurse and Pierce Pickpurse call upon God at the last (1147 ff.), there is no assurance that their prayer is answered. The stern social fable seems forbiddingly deterministic. The doctrine that the young must be trained because older men are (perhaps fatally) set in their ways becomes in *Like Will* a counsel of pessimism—the unregenerate can only wonder if things might have been different had they been properly educated. Now they are irredeemably fixed in their manner of life (1010, 1140). The pessimistic view of society in this play cuts another way as well— at the end evil continues to exist not only in Nichol Newfangle (who has escaped with only a comic beating) but also in several of the unregenerate. The play examines a corrupt society rather than offering a programme for its correction.

As you are, such is your reward—this teaching of the play is reflected in the fates of both the virtuous and the vicious. The rewards of virtue are immediate; Good Fame and Honour crown Virtuous Life as soon as his steadfastness has been shown by rejecting Nichol Newfangle. The wages of sin as the play presents them are slower in coming but no less inevitable. Nichol Newfangle makes this clear by promising patrimonies and bequests to the evil-doers, and these gifts turn out to be what the recipients truly deserve. We perceive and enjoy the irony, laughing at the jokes with Nichol Newfangle.

Like Will has many proverbs which (like the course of the action) suggest that the vice and virtue groups are each closely knit but are impossibly distant from each other. The contrasted groups of social types and representative figures follow separate courses and the conversion to virtue of a vice is only mocked by

Nichol (685 ff.). The virtuous are ignorant of the vicious life, as is shown by Virtuous Life's opinion, 'The vicious hath consciences so heavy as lead;/Their conscience and their doing is always at strife' (681–2). Actually, such pangs of conscience are not shown until vices are defeated and suffering: the only time conscience is mentioned (to Tom Collier) is in a joking question (160–1). Within each group, camaraderie and friendship are common— the Tom Collier episode, for example, serves only to show that a fit mate can be found for anyone.

Remembering the traditionally seductive function of the vices, one wonders why the Vice is central in *Like Will*, where clearly the unregenerate have always been as we see them. Further, is the Vice a seducer at all, or just a master of ceremonies? Nichol does not seem to be completely a member of the vice-party—he inflicts punishment with Severity and is often very ironic about his fellows. Yet the two successive groups of defeated type figures attempt to depict Nichol as an enticer. Rafe warns him against enticing 'any more young men' (1040). Cutbert Cutpurse later waxes eloquent on Nichol as the bower of iniquity, evil company, and so on (1129–39) although the accusations are not fully borne out by the action. The various groups of thieves and ruffians came to Nichol, not he to them. They were already evil when they entered, greeting the Vice as an old friend; they appear evil as a result of upbringing or else perhaps seduced by the Vice before the play opens. Once they come to Nichol, however, they are dominated by him. He sardonically greets and dismisses the various groups, and in his hands their time on stage becomes a series of games which he plays with them for our benefit. While not a tempter, Nichol is a catalyst. He gives false hopes of land and wealth, and well realizes that this will lead evil men into recklessness and defeat. As Ben Jonson put it, 'men may securely sin, but safely never': Nichol gives such false 'security'.

The narrowing of focus upon social types allows Fulwell to present moral defeat and death as the horrifying results of evil. The play centres upon evil—all but a small part is concerned with it—and Nichol's survival, sardonic and victorious, is a final honest lesson. In contrast with *Mankind*, *Like Will* shows how evil defiles and finally triumphs over those who dally with it. The interluders' concern with man's nature and society's imperatives— their 'moral vision'—is apparent in these plays, and was to flower in the greater dramas soon to be written for the London theatres.

BIBLIOGRAPHY

Bernard, J. E., *The Prosody of the Tudor Interlude* (1939).
Bevington, D. M., *From 'Mankind' to Marlowe* (Cambridge, Mass., 1962).
Contains a useful list of plays.
— *Tudor Drama and Politics* (Cambridge, Mass., 1968).
Bolwell, R., *The Life and Works of John Heywood* (New York, 1921).
Chambers, E. K., *The Medieval Stage*. 2 vols. (London, 1903).
Coogan, Sr. Phillippa, *An Interpretation of the Moral Play 'Mankind'* (Washington, 1947).
Craig, Hardin, *English Religious Drama* (Oxford, 1955).
Craik, T. W., *The Tudor Interlude* (Leicester, 1962).
Cushman, L. B., *The Devil and the Vice in the English Dramatic Literature Before Shakespeare* (Halle, 1900).
Eccles, Mark (ed.), *The Macro Plays*. Early English Text Society, No. 262 (London, 1969).
Hogrefe, Pearl, *The Sir Thomas More Circle* (Urbana, Illinois, 1969).
Johnson, R. C., *John Heywood* (New York, 1970).
MacKenzie, W. Roy, *The English Moralities from the Point of View of Allegory* (Boston, 1914).
Murray, J. T., *English Dramatic Companies, 1558–1642* (London, 1910).
Nicoll, Allardyce, *Masks, Mimes, and Miracles* (London, 1931).
Nosworthy, J. M. (ed.), *Lusty Juventus*. Malone Society Reprints (London, 1971).
Ramsay, R. L. (ed.), *John Skelton's Magnificence*. Early English Text Society, Extra Series, No. 98 (London, 1906).
Reed, A. W., *Early Tudor Drama* (London, 1926).
Ribner, Irving, 'Ulpian Fulwell and his Family', *Notes and Queries*, cxcv (1950), 444–8.
— 'Ulpian Fulwell and the Court of High Commission', *Notes and Queries*, cxcvi (1961), 268–70.
Rossiter, A. P. *English Drama from Early Times to the Elizabethans* (1950).
Smart, W. K., 'Some Notes on *Mankind*', *Modern Philology*, xiv (1916–17), 45–58, 293–313.
Spivack, Bernard, *Shakespeare and the Allegory of Evil* (New York, 1958).
Wilson, F. P., *The English Drama 1485–1585* (Oxford, 1969). Contains a helpful general bibliography by G. K. Hunter.

MANKIND

[Enter Mercy]

he very founder and beginner of our first creation
g us sinful wretches he oweth to be magnified,
for our disobedience he had none indignation
nd his own son to be torn and crucified.
obsequious service to him should be applied,
ere he was Lord of all and made all thing of naught
the sinful sinner to had him revived,
d for his redemption set his own son at naught.
may be said and verified mankind was dear bought;
y the piteous death of Jesu he had his remedy.   10
He was purged of his defaut that wretchedly had wrought
By His glorious passion, that blessed lavatory.
O sovereigns, I beseech you your conditions to rectify,
And with humility and reverence to have a remotion
To this blessed prince that our nature doth glorify,
That ye may be participable of his retribution.
I have be the very mean for your restitution:
Mercy is my name, that mourneth for your offence.
Divert not yourself in time of temptation
That ye may be acceptable to God at your going hence.   20
The great mercy of God that is of most preeminence,
By mediation of Our Lady that is ever abundant
To the sinful creature that will repent his negligence.
I pray God at your most need that Mercy be your defendant.
In good works I avise you, sovereigns, to be perseverant,
To purify your souls that they be not corrupt;
For your ghostly enmy will make his avaunt
Your good conditions if he may interrupt.
O ye sovereigns that sit and ye brothern that stand right up,
Prick not your felicities in things transitory.   30
Behold not the earth, but lift your eye up;
See how the head the members daily do magnify.
Who is the head forsooth I shall you certify:
I mean Our Saviour, that was likened to a lamb,
And his saints be the members that daily He doth satisfy

[Mankind

DRAMATIS PERSONAE

Mankind
Mercy
Mischief
New Guise ⎫
Naught ⎬ *vices*
Nowadays ⎭
Titivillus, *a devil*]

With the precious river than runneth from his womb.
There is none such food by water nor by lond,
So precious, so glorious, so needful to our intent,
For it hath dissolved mankind from the bitter bond
Of the mortal enmy, that venemous serpent, 40
From the which God preserve you all at the last Judgement!
For sickerly there shall be a strait examination:
The corn shall be saved, the chaff shall be brent.
I beseech you heartily, have this premeditation.

[Enter Mischief]

Mis. I beseech you heartily, leave your calc'ation,
Leave your chaff, leave your corn, leave your dalliation;
Your wit is little, your head is mickle, ye are full of
But sir, I pray this question to clarify: predication.
Mish mash, driff, draff,
Some was corn and some was chaff 50
My dame said my name was Raff;
Unshut your lock and take an halpenny.
Mercy. Why come ye hither, brother? Ye were not desired.
Mis. For a winter corn-thresher, sir, I have hired;
And ye said the corn should be saved and the chaff should
be fired,
And he proveth nay, as it show'th by this verse:
'Corn servit breadibus, chaff horsibus, straw firibusque.'
This is as much to say, to your lewd understanding,
As the corn shall serve to bread at the next baking.
'Chaff horsibus, et reliqua.' 60
The chaff to horse shall be good provent,
When a man is forcold the straw may be brent,
And so forth, &c.
Mercy. Avoid, good brother, ye ben culpable
To interrupt thus my talking delectable.
Mis. Sir, I have nother horse nor saddle,
Therefore I may not ride.
Mercy. Hie you forth on foot brother, in God's name!
Mis. I say, sir, I am come hither to make you game.
Yet bade ye me not go out in the Deul's name, 70
And I will abide.

27

[*A leaf (originally the second) of the ms. is missing here, which
contained about eighty lines. At the accidental mention of their
names (cf. 111) New Guise, Naught, and Nowadays have entered
to join in taunting Mercy.*]

[*New.*] And how, minstrels, play the common trace.
    Lay on with thy baleis till his belly brest.
Naught. I put case I break my neck. How than?
New. I give no force, by Saint Anne.
Now. Leap about lively! Thou art a wight man.
    Let us be merry while we be here.
Naught. Shall I break my neck to show you sport?
Now. Therefore ever beware of thy report.
Naught. I beshrew ye all, here is a shrewd sort;   80
    Have thereat then with a merry cheer.

Here they dance. Mercy saith:

Do way, do way this rule, sirs, do way.
Now. Do way, good Adam, do way?
    This is no part of thy play.
Naught. Yes, marry, I pray you, for I love not this revelling.
    Come forth, good father, I you pray,
    By a little ye may assay.
    Anon, off with your clothes, if ye will play;
    Go to, for I have had a pretty scuttling.
Mercy. Nay, brother, I will not dance.   90
New. If ye will, sir, my brother will make you to prance.
Now. With all my heart, sir, if I may you avance,
    Ye may assay by a little trace.
Naught. Yea, sir, will ye do well?
    Trace not with them by my counsel,
    For I have traced somewhat too fell;
    I tell it is a narrow space.
    But sir, I trow of us three I heard you speak.
New. Christ's curse had therefore, for I was in sleep.
Now. And I had the cup ready in my hand, ready to go to   100
    Therefore, sir, curtly greet you well.   meat;
Mercy. Few words, few and well set!
New. Sir, it is the new guise and the new jet,
    Many words and shortly set,
    This is the new guise, every-deal.

Mercy. Lady, help! How wretches delight in their simple ways.
Now. Say not again the new guise nowadays.
Thou shall find us shrews at all assays.
Beware! Ye may soon like a buffet.
Mercy. He was well occupied that brought you brethern.   110
Naught. I heard you call New Guise, Nowadays, Naught, all
    these three together;
If ye say that I lie, I shall make you to slither.
Lo, take you here a trippet.
Mercy. Say me your names, I know you not.
New. New Guise, I.
[*Now.*]   I, Nowadays.
[*Naught.*]   I, Naught.
Mercy. By Jesu Christ that me dear bought
Ye betray many men.
New. Betray? Nay, nay, sir, nay, nay!
We make them both fresh and gay.
But of your name, sir, I you pray,   120
That we may you ken.
Mercy. Mercy is my name and my denomination.
I conceive ye have but a little favour in my communication.
New. Ey, ey! Your body is full of English Latin.
To have this English made in Latin
I am afeard it will burst:
    'Pravo te quod the butcher unto me
    When I stole a leg o' mutton.'
Ye are a strong cunning clerk.
Now. I pray you heartily, worshipful clerk: 130
    'I have eaten a dishful of curds
    And I have shitten your mouth full of turds.'
Now open your satchel with Latin words
And say me this in clerical manner!
Also,
    'I have a wife, her name is Rachel
    Betwix her and me was a great battle.
    And fain of you I would hear tell
    Who was the most master.'
Naught. Thy wife, Rachel, I dare lay twenty lies.
Now. Who spake to thee, fool? Thou art not wise.   140
Go and do that 'longeth to thine office:
Osculare fundamentum.

Naught. Lo, master, lo, here is a pardon belly-met:
  It is granted of Pope Pocket,
  If ye will put your nose in his wife's socket
  Ye shall have forty days of pardon.
Mercy. This idle language ye shall repent;
  Out of this place I would ye went.
New. Go we hence all three with one assent;
  My father is irk of our eloquence,   150
  Therefore I will no longer tarry.
  God bring you, master, and Blessed Mary
  To the number of the demonical friary.
Now. Come wind, come rain,
  Though I come never again,
  The Deul put out both your eyn!
  Fellows, go we hence tight.
Naught. Go we hence, a Deul way,
  Here is the door, here is the way.
  Farewell, gentle Jeffrey,   160
  I pray God give you good night.

                    Exiant simul. Cantent.

Mercy. Thanked be God, we have a fair deliverance
  Of these three unthrifty guests.
  They know full little what is their ordinance.
  I prove by reason they be worse than beasts.
  A beast doth after his natural institution:
  Ye may conceive by their disport and behavour,
  Their joy and delight is in derision
  Of their own Christ, to His dishonour.
  This condition of living, it is prejudicial;   170
  Beware thereof, it is worse than any felony or treason.
  How may it be excused before the Justice of all,
  When for every idle word we must yield a reason?
  They have great ease, therefore they will take no thought.
  But how then, when the angel of heaven shall blow the trump
  And say to the transgressors that wickedly hath wrought
  'Come forth unto your Judge and yield your account?'
  Then shall I, Mercy, begin sore to weep;
  Nother comfort nor counsel there shall none be had,
  But such as they have sown, such shall they reap.   180
  They be wanton now, but then shall they be sad.

The good new guise, nowadays, I will not disallow.
I discommend the vicious guise; I pray have me excused,
I need not to speak of it, your reason will tell it you:
Take that is to be taken, and leave that is to be refused.

[Enter Mankind]

Man. Of the earth and of the clay we have our propagation;
By the providence of God, thus be we derivate,
To whose mercy I recommend this whole congregation:
I hope unto his bliss ye be all predestinate.
Every man for his degree I trust shall be participate,   190
If we will mortify our carnal condition
And our voluntary desires, that ever be perversionate;
To renounce them and yield us under God's provision.
My name is Mankind. I have my composition
Of a body and of a soul, of condition contrary.
Betwix them twain is a great division;
He that should be subject, now he hath the victory.
This is to me a lamentable story,
To see my flesh of my soul to have governance.
Where the goodwife is master, the goodman may be sorry.   200
I may both syth and sob, this is a piteous remembrance.
O thou my soul, so subtle in thy substance,
Alas, what was thy fortune and thy chance
To be associate with my flesh, that stinking dunghill?
Lady, help! Sovereigns, it doth my soul much ill
To see the flesh prosperous and the soul trodden underfote.
I shall go to yonder man, and assay him I will;
I trust of ghostly solace he will be my bote.
All hail, seemly father! Ye be welcome to this house.
Of the very wisdom ye have participation.   210
My body with my soul is ever querelous;
I pray you, for Saint Charity, of your supportation.
I beseech you heartily of your ghostly comfort;
I am unsteadfast in living; my name is Mankind.
My ghostly enmy the Deul will have a great disport
In sinful guiding if he may see me end.
Mercy. Christ send you good comfort! Ye be welcome, my friend.
Stand up on your feet, I pray you arise.
My name is Mercy; ye be to me full hend.
To eschew vice I will you avise.   220

31

Man. O Mercy, of all grace and virtue ye are the well.
I have heard tell of right worshipful clerks
Ye be approximate to God, and near of his counsel;
He hath institute you above all his works.
Oh, your lovely words to my soul are sweeter than honey.
Mercy. The temptation of the flesh ye must resist like a man,
For there is ever a battle betwix the soul and the body:
'Vita hominis est milicia super terram.'
Oppress your ghostly enmy and be Christ's own knight;
Be never a coward again your adversary.   230
If ye will be crowned, ye must needs fight:
Intend well, and God will be your adjutory.
Remember, my friend, the time of continuance,
So help me God, it is but a cherry time.
Spend it well; serve God with heart's affiance.
Distemper not your brain with good ale nor with wine.
Measure is treasure, I forbid you not the use:
Measure yourself ever; beware of excess,
The superfluous guise I will that ye refuse.
When nature is sufficed, anon that ye cease.   240
If a man have an horse, and keep him not too high,
He may then rule him at his own desire:
If he be fed over-well he will disobey
And in hap cast his master in the mire.
New. Ye say true, sir, ye are no faitour:
I have fed my wife so well till she is my master.
I have a great wound on my head, lo, and thereon layeth
And another there, I piss my peson.   a plaster.
And my wife were your horse, she would you all to-ban;
Ye feed your horse in measure, ye are a wise man.   250
I trow, and ye were the king's palfreyman,
A good horse should be gesoun.
Man. Where speaks this fellow? Will he not come near?
Mercy. All to soon, my brother, I fear me, for yow.
He was here right now, by him that bought me dear,
With other of his fellows. They can much sorrow.
They will be here right soon, if I out depart.
Think on my doctrine; it shall be your defence.
Learn while I am here; set my words in heart.
Within a short space I must needs hence.   260
Now. The sooner the lever, and it be even anon!

I trow your name is Do Little, ye be so long fro home;
If ye would go hence, we shall come everychon,
Mo than a good sort.
Ye have leave I dare well say,
When ye will, go forth your way;
Men have little daint of your play
Because ye make no sport.

Naught. Your pottage shall be forcold, sir; when will ye go dine? 270
I have seen a man lost twenty nobles in as little time;
Yet it was not I, by Saint Quentin,
For I was never worth a potful o' worts sithen I was born.
My name is Naught, I love well to make merry.
I have be sithen with the common tapster of Bury,
And played so long the fool that I am even very weary;
Yet shall I be there again to-morn.

Mercy. I have much care for you, my own friend.
Your enmies will be here anon; they make their avaunt.
Think well in your heart your name is Mankind:
Be not unkind to God, I pray you be His servant. 280
Be steadfast in condition, see ye be not variant.
Lose not thorough folly that is bought so dear.
God will prove you soon, and if that ye be constant,
Of His bliss perpetual ye shall be partener.
Ye may not have your intent at your first desire.
See the great patience of Job in tribulation;
Like as the smith trieth iron in the fire,
So was he tried by God's visitation.
He was of your nature and of your fragility;
Follow the steps of him, my own sweet son, 290
And say as he said in your trouble and adversity:
'Dominus dedit, dominus abstulit; sicut sibi placuit,
ita factum est; nomen Domini benedictum!'
Moreover, in special I give you in charge,
Beware of New Guise, Nowadays, and Naught.
Nice in their array, in language they be large;
To pervert your conditions all the means shall be sought.
Good son, intromit not yourself in their company.
They heard not a mass this twelmoneth, I dare well say.
Give them none audience; they will tell you many a lie. 300
Do truly your labour and keep your holiday.
Beware of Titivillus, for he loseth no way,

33

That goeth invisible and will not be sen.
He will round in your ear and cast a net before your eye.
He is worst of them all; God let him never then!
If ye displease God, ask mercy anon,
Else Mischief will be ready to brace you in his bridle.
Kiss me now, my dear darling. God shield you from your fon!
Do truly your labour and be never idle.
The blessing of God be with you and with all these
    worshipful men!   310

[*Exit Mercy*]

Man. Amen, for Saint Charity, amen!
    Now blessed be Jesu! My soul is well satiate
    With the mellifluous doctrine of this worshipful man.
    The rebellion of my flesh now it is superate.
    Thanked be God of the coming that I came.
    Here will I sit and title in this paper
    The incomparable estate of my promition.
    Worshipful sovereigns, I have written here
    The glorious remembrance of my noble condition.
    To have remos and memory of myself thus written it is,   320
    To defend me from all superstitious charms:
    'Memento, homo, quod cinis es, et in cinerem reverteris.'
    Lo I bear on my breast the badge of mine arms.
New. The weather is cold, God send us good feris!
    'Cum sancto sanctus eris et cum perverso perverteris.
    Ecce quam bonum et quam jocundum,' quod the Deul to
    'Habitare fratres in unum.'   the freris,
Man. I hear a fellow speak; with him I will not mell:
    This earth with my spade I shall assay to delf;
    To eschew idleness, I do it mine own self.   330
    I pray God send it his fusion!

[*Enter the vices*]

Now. Make room, sirs, for we have be long,
    We will come give you a Christmas song.
Naught. Now I pray all the yemandry that is here
    To sing with us with a merry cheer:

    It is written with a coal, yt is written with a coal,
New. and Now. It is written with a coal, it is written &c

34

Naught. He that shitteth with his hole, he that shitteth with
   his hole,
New. [*and*] *Now.* He that shitteth with his hole &c.
Naught. But he wipe his arse clean, but he &c.   340
New. [*and*] *Now.* But he wipe his arse clean, but he &c.
Naught. On his breech it shall be seen, on his breech &c.
New. [*and*] *Now.* On his breech it shall be seen, on his &c.
Cantent Omnes. Holike, holike, holike, holike, holike, holike!

New. Ey Mankind, God speed you with your spade!
   I shall tell you of a marriage:
   I would your mouth and his arse that this made
   Were married jointly together!
Man. Hie you hence fellows, with breding;
   Leave your derision and your japing.   350
   I must needs labour, it is my living.
Now. What, sir, we came but late hither.
   Shall all this corn grow here
   That ye shall have the next year?
   If it be so, corn had need be dear,
   Else ye shall have a poor life.
Naught. Alas, good father, this labour fretteth you to the bone.
   But for your crop I take great moan.
   Ye shall never spend it alone;
   I shall assay to get you a wife.   360
   How many acres suppose ye here by estimation?
New. Ey, how ye turn the earth up and down!
   I have be in my days in many good town
   Yet saw I never such another tilling.
Man. Why stand ye idle? It is pity that ye were born!
Now. We shall bargain with you and nother mock nor scorn.
   Take a good cart in harvest and load it with your corn,
   And what shall we give you for the leaving?
Naught. He is a good stark labourer, he would fain do well.
   He hath met with the good man Mercy in a shrewd cell.   370
   For all this he may have many a hungry meal.
   Yet will ye see he is politic:
   Here shall be good corn, he may not miss it;
   If he will have rain he may overpiss it:
   And if he will have compass he may overbliss it
   A little with his arse like.

35

Man. Go and do your labour! God let you never thee!
   Or with my spade I shall you ding, by the Holy Trinity!
   Have ye none other man to mock, but ever me?
   Ye would have me of your set?   380
   Hie you forth lively, for hence I will you drife.
New. Alas my jewels! I shall be shent of my wife!
Now. Alas! and I am like never for to thrive,
   I have such a buffet.
Man. Hence I say, New Guise, Nowadays, and Naught!
   It was said before, all the means should be sought
   To pervert my conditions and bring me to naught.
   Hence thieves! Ye have made many a leasing.
Naught. Marry I was forcold, but now am I warm.
   Ye are evil avised, sir, for ye have done harm.   390
   By Cock's body sacred, I have such a pain in my arm
   I may not change a man a farthing.
Man. Now I thank God, kneeling on my knee.
   Blessed be his name, he is of high degree.
   By the subsidy of his grace that he hath sent me
   Three of mine enmies I have put to flight.
   Yet this instrument, sovereigns, is not made to defend.
   David saith, 'Nec in hasta nec in gladio salvat Dominus.'
Naught. No, marry I beshrew you, it is in spadibus!
   Therefore Christ's curse come on your headibus   400
   To send you less might!   *Exiant.*
Man. I promise you these fellows will no more come here,
   For some of them, certainly, were somewhat too near.
   My father Mercy avised me to be of a good cheer
   And again my enmies manly for to fight.
   I shall convict them, I hope, everychon.
   Yet I say amiss—I do it not alone.
   With the help of the grace of God I resist my fon
   And their malicious heart.
   With my spade I will depart, my worshipful sovereigns,   410
   And live ever with labour to correct my insolence.
   I shall go fet corn for my land, I pray you of patience;
   Right soon I shall revert.

   [Exit Mankind. Enter Mischief]

Mis. Alas, alas, that ever I was wrought!
   Alas the while, I worse than naught!

Sithen I was here, by him that me bought,
I am utterly undone!
I, Mischief, was here at the beginning of the game
And argued with Mercy, God give him shame!
He hath taught Mankind, while I have be vain,   420
To fight manly again his fon;
For with his spade, that was his weapon,
New Guise, Nowadays, Naught hath all to-beaten.
I have great pity to see them weepin'.
Will ye list? I hear them cry.

[Enter the Vices] Clamant.

Alas, alas! Come hither, I shall be your borrow.
Alack, alack! Ven, ven! Come hither with sorrow!
Peace, fair babies, ye shall have an apple tomorrow!
Why greet ye so, why?
New. Alas, master, alas! My privite!   430
Mis. Ah, where? Alack! Fair babe, ba me!
Abide; too soon I shall it see.
Now. Here, here, see my head, good master!
Mis. Lady, help! Seely darling, ven ven!
I shall help thee of thy pain;
I shall smite off thy head and set it on again.
Naught. By our Lady, sir, a fair plaster!
Will ye off with his head? It is a shrewd charm!
As for me, I have none harm.
I were loath to forbear mine arm.   440
Ye play in nomine patris, chop!
New. Ye shall not chop my jewels, and I may.
Now. Yea, Christ's cross, will ye smite my head away?
There were one and one! Out! Ye shall not assay;
I might well be called a fop.
Mis. I can chop it off and make it again.
New. I had a shrewd recumbentibus but I feel no pain.
Now. And my head is all safe and whole again.
Now, touching the matter of Mankind,
Let us have an interlection, sithen ye be come hither.   450
It were good to have an end.
Mis. How, how, a minstrel! know ye any aught?
Naught. I can pipe in a Walsingham whistle, I, Naught, Naught.
Mis. Blow apace, and thou shall bring him in with a flute.

37

Tit. I come with my legs under me.

Mis. How, New Guise, Nowadays, hark or I go;
   When our heads were together I spake of 'si dedero'.

New. Yea, go thy way! We shall gather money unto,
   Else there shall no man him see.

[*Exit Mischief*]

Now, ghostly to our purpose, worshipful sovereigns,   460
We intend to gather money, if it please your negligence,
For a man with a head that is of great omnipotence.

Now. Keep your tale, in goodness I pray you, good brother!
   He is a worshipful man, sirs, saving your reverence;
   He loveth no groats, nor pence of two pence,
   Give us red rials if ye will see his abominable presence.

New. Not so! Ye that mow not pay the ton, pay the tother.
   At the goodman of this house first we will assay.
   God bless you, master. Ye say as ill, yet ye will not say nay.
   Let us go by and by and do them pay.   470
   Ye pay all alike; well mut ye fare!

Naught. I say, New Guise, Nowadays, estis vos pecuniatus?
   I have cried a fair while, I beshrew your patus.

Now. Ita vere, magister. Come forth now your gatus!
   He is a goodly man, sirs, make space and beware!

[*Enter Titivillus*]

Tit. Ego sum dominancium dominus, and my name is Titivillus.
   Ye that have good horse, to you I say caveatis:
   Here is an able fellowship to trice him out at your gatus.

(*Loquitur ad New Guise*)

Ego probo sic: sir New Guise, lend me a penny.

New. I have a great purse, sir, but I have no money.   480
   By the mass, I fail two farthings of an halpenny;
   Yet had I ten pound this night that was.

Tit. (*Loquitur ad Nowadays*) What is in thy purse? Thou art a
   stout fellow.

Now. The Deul have the whit, I am a clean gentleman;
   I pray God I be never worse stored than I am.
   It shall be otherwise, I hope, or this night pass.

Tit. (*Loquitur ad Naught*) Hark now! I say thou hast many a
   penny.

Naught. Non nobis domine, non nobis, by Saint Denys,
   The Deul may dance in my purse for any penny,
   It is as clean as a bird's arse.   490
Tit. Now I say yet again, caveatis!
   Here is an able fellowship to trice him out of your gatus.
   Now I say, New Guise, Nowadays, and Naught,
   Go and search the country, anon it be sought,
   Some here, some there; what if ye may catch aught?
   If ye fail of horse, take what ye may else.
New. Then speak to Mankind for the recumbentibus of my
     jewels.
Now. Remember my broken head in the worship of the five
Naught. Yea, good sir, and the scitica in my arm.   vowels.
Tit. I know full well what Mankind did to you.   500
   Mischief hath informed of all the matter through,
   I shall venge your quarrel, I make God a vow.
   Forth, and espy where ye may do harm.
   Take William Fide, if ye will have any mo.
   I say New Guise, whither art thou avised to go?
New. First I shall begin at Master Huntington of Sawston,
   Fro thence I shall go to William Thurlay of Hauxton,
   And so forth to Pichard of Trumpington.
   I will keep me to these three.
Now. I shall go to William Baker of Walton,   510
   To Richard Bollman of Gayton;
   I shall spare Master Wood of Fullbourn,
   He is a noli me tangere.
Naught. I shall go to William Patrick of Massingham,
   I shall spare Master Alington of Bottisham,
   And Hammond of Swaffham,
   For dread of in manus tuas queck.
   Fellows, come forth, and go we hence together.
New. Sith we shall go, let us be well ware whether;
   If we may be take, we come no more hether.   520
   Let us con well our neck-verse, that we have not a check.
Tit. Go your way a Deul way, go your way all;
   I bless you with my left hand: foul you befall!
   Come again, I warn, as soon as I you call,
   And bring your avantage into this place.

[*Exit the Vices*]

To speak with Mankind, I will tarry here this tide,
And assay his good purpose for to set aside.
The good man Mercy shall no longer be his guide;
I shall make him to dance another trace.
Ever I go invisible, it is my jet,   530
And before his eye thus I will hang my net
To blench his sight; I hope to have his foot-met.
To irk him of his labour I shall make a frame:
This board shall be hid under the earth privily;
His spade shall enter, I hope, unreadily;
By then he hath assayed, he shall be very angry
And lose his patience, pain of shame.
I shall menge his corn with drawk and with darnel;
It shall not be like to sow nor to sell.
Yonder he cometh; I pray of counsel: 540
He shall ween grace were wane.

[*Enter Mankind*]

Man. Now God of his mercy send us of his sand!
I have brought seed here to sow with my land;
While I overdilew it, here it shall stand.
In nomine Patris et Filii et Spiritus Sancti. Now I will begin.
This land is so hard it maketh unlusty and irk;
I shall sow my corn at winter, and let God work.
Alas, my corn is lost! Here is a foul work.
I see well by tilling little shall I win;
Here I give up my spade for now and for ever.   550

Here Titivillus goeth out with the spade.

To occupy my body I will not put me in dever;
I will hear my evensong here or I dissever.
This place I assign as for my kirk;
Here in my kirk I kneel on my knees:
Pater noster qui es in coelis.

[*Enter Titivillus*]

Tit. I promise you I have no lead on my heels;
I am here again to make this fellow irk.
Whist! Peace! I shall go to his ear and tittle therein.
A short prayer thirleth Heaven; of thy prayer blin;
Thou art holier than ever was any of thy kin;   560

Arise and avent thee, nature compels.

Man. I will into the yard, sovereigns, and come again soon,
For dread of the colic and eke of the stone,
I will go do that needs must be done.
My beads shall be here for whosomever will else.   *Exiat.*

Tit. Mankind was busy in his prayer, yet I did him arise.
He is conveyed, by Christ, from his divine service.
Whither is he, trow ye? Iwis I am wonder wise;
I have sent him forth to shit leasings.
If ye have any silver, in hap pure brass,   570
Take a little powder of Paris and cast over his face,
And even in the owl-flight let him pass.
Titivillus can learn you many pretty things!
I trow Mankind will come again sone,
Or else I fear me evensong will be done.
His beads shall be triced aside, and that anon.
Ye shall a good sport if ye will abide;
Mankind cometh again, well fare he;
I shall answer him ad omnia quaere.
There shall be set abroach a clerical matter.   580
I hope of his purpose to set him aside.

[*Enter Mankind*]

Man. Evensong hath be in the saying, I trow, a fair while;
I am irk of it; it is too long by one mile.
Do way! I will no more so oft over the church stile.
Be as be may, I shall do another.
Of labour and prayer, I am near irk of both;
I will no more of it, though Mercy be wroth.
My head is very heavy, I tell you forsoth;
I shall sleep full my belly and he were my brother.

Tit. And ever ye did, for me keep now your silence;   590
Not a word, I charge you, pain of forty pence,
A pretty game shall be showed you or ye go hence.
Ye may hear him snore, he is sad asleep.
Whist! Peace! The Deul is dead! I shall go round in his ear.
Alas, Mankind, alas! Mercy stol'n a mare;
He is run away fro his master, there wot no man where;
Moreover, he stole both a horse and a net.
But yet I heard say he brake his neck as he rode in France;
But I think he rideth over the gallows, to learn for to dance,

41

Because of his theft; that is his governance.   600
Trust no more on him, he is a marred man.
Mickle sorrow with thy spade before thou hast wrought.
Arise and ask mercy of New Guise, Nowadays and Naught.
They can avise thee for the best; let their goodwill be sought,
And thy own wife brethel and take thee a leman.
Farewell, everychon! For I have done my game,
For I have brought Mankind to mischief and to shame.

[Exit Titivillus]

Man. Whoop ho! Mercy hath broken his neckercher, avows,
  Or he hangeth by the neck high upon the gallows.
  Adieu, fair masters! I will haste me to the ale-house   610
  And speak with New Guise, Nowadays, and Naught,
  And get me a leman with a smattering face.

[Enter New Guise]

New. Make space, for Cock's body sacred, make space!
  Ah ha! Well overrun! God give him evil grace!
  We were near Saint Patrick's way, by him that me bought.
  I was twitched by the neck; the game was begun;
  A grace was, the halter brast asunder: ecce signum!
  The half is about my neck; we had a near run!
  'Beware' quod the goodwife when she smote off her
      husband's head, 'beware!'
  Mischief is a convict, for he conned his neck-verse.   620
  My body gave a swing when I hung upon the case.
  Alas, he will hang such a lighly man, and a fierce,
  For stealing of an horse, I pray God give him care!
  Do way this halter. What Deul doth Mankind here, with
  Alas, how my neck is sore, I make a vow!   sorrow?
Man. Ye be welcome, New Guise. Sir, what cheer with you?
New. Well, sir, I have no cause to mourn.
Man. What was that about your neck, so God you amend?
New. In faith, Saint Audrey's holy bend.
  I have a little dishes as it please God to send,   630
  With a running ringworm.

[Enter Nowadays]

Now. Stand aroom, I pray thee brother mine!
  I have laboured all this night; when shall we go dine?

A church here beside shall pay for ale, bread, and wine;
Lo, here is stuff will serve.
New. Now by the holy Mary, thou art better marchand than I!

[Enter Naught]

Naught. Avaunt knaves, let me go by!
I cannot get and I should starve.

[Enter Mischief]

Mis. Here cometh a man of arms! Why stand ye so still?
Of murder and manslaughter I have my belly-fill.   640
Now. What Mischief, have ye been in prison? And it be your
Me seemeth ye have scoured a pair of fetters.   will,
Mis. I was chained by the arms: lo, I have them here;
The chains I brast asunder and killed the gaoler,
Yea, and his fair wife halsed in a corner;
Ah, how sweetly I kissed the sweet mouth of hers!
When I had do I was mine own butler,
I brought away with me both dish and doubler.
Here is enow for me; be of good cheer,
Yet well fare the new chesance!   650
Man. I ask mercy of New Guise, Nowadays, and Naught.
Once with my spade I remember that I fought;
I will make you amends if I hurt you aught
Or did any grievance.
New. What a Deul liketh thee to be of this disposition?
Man. I dreamt Mercy was hang, this was my vision,
And that to you three I should have recourse and remotion.
Now I pray you heartily of your good will;
I cry you mercy of all that I did amiss.
Now. I say, New Guise, Naught, Titivillus made all this: 660
As sicker as God is in heaven, so it is.
Naught. Stand up on your feet! Why stand ye so still?
New. Master Mischief, we will you exhort
Mankind's name in your book for to report.
Mis. I will not so, I will set a court.
Nowadays, make proclamation,
And do it sub forma juris, dasard!
Now. Oyet! Oyet! Oyet! All manner of men and common
To the court of Mischief other come or sen!   women
Mankind shall return; he is one of our men.   670

43

Mis. Naught, come forth, thou shall be steward.
New. Master Mischief, his side gown may be tolled;
　He may have a jacket thereof, and money told.

Naught Scribit.

Man. I will do for the best, so I have no cold;
　Hold I pray you, and take it with you,
　And let me have it again in any wise.
New. I promise you a fresh jacket after the new guise.
Man. Go and do that 'longeth to your office,
　And spare that ye mow!

[*Exit New Guise*]

Naught. Hold, Master Mischief, and read this.   680
Mis. Here is blottibus in blottis,
　Blottorum blottibus istis.
　I beshrew your ears, a fair hand!
Now. Yea, it is a good running fist.
　Such an hand may not be missed.
Naught. I should have done better, had I wist.
Mis. Take heed, sirs, it stood you on hand.
　'Carici tenta generalis
　In a place there good ale is
　Anno regni regitalis   690
　Edwardi nullateni
　On yestern day in Feverere'—the year passeth fully
　As Naught hath written; here is our Tully;
　'Anno regni regis nulli!'
Now. What ho, New Guise! Thou makest much tarrying;
　That jacket shall not be worth a farthing.

[*Enter New Guise*]

New. Out of my way, sirs, for dread of fighting!
　Lo here is a feat tail, light to leap about!
Naught. It is not shapen worth a morsel of bread;
　There is too much cloth, it weighs as any lead;   700
　I shall go and mend it, else I will lose my head.
　Make space sirs, let me go out.

[*Exit Naught*]

Mis. Mankind, come hither! God send you the gout!
　Ye shall go to all the good fellows in the country about;

44

Unto the goodwife when the goodman is out.
'I will', say ye.
Man.   I will, sir.
New. There are but six deadly sins, lechery is none,
  As it may be verified by us brethels everychon.
  Ye shall go rob, steal, and kill, as fast as ye may gone.   710
  'I will', say ye.
Man.   I will, sir.
Now. On Sundays on the morrow early betime
  Ye shall with us to the ale-house early to go dine
  And forbear Mass and Matins, Hours and Prime.
  'I will', say ye.
Man.   I will, sir.
Mis. Ye must have by your side a long da pacem,
  As true men ride by the way for to unbrace them,
  Take their money, cut their throats, thus overface them.   720
  'I will', say ye.
Man.   I will, sir.

[*Enter Naught*]

Naught. Here is a jolly jacket! How say ye?
New. It is a good jack of fence for a man's body.
  Hay, dog, hay! Whoop ho! Go your way lightly!
  Ye are well made for to run.
Mis. Tidings, tidings! I have espied one!
  Hence with your stuff, fast we were gone!
  I beshrew the last shall come to his home.
Dicant Omnes. Amen!   730

[*Enter Mercy*]

Mercy. What ho, Mankind! Flee that fellowship, I you pray!
Man. I shall speak with thee another time, to-morn or the
        next day.
  We shall go forth together to keep my father's year-day.
  A tapster, a tapster! Stow, statt, stow!
Mis. A mischief go with thee! Here I have a foul fall.
  Hence, away fro me, or I shall beshit you all.
New. What ho, hostler, hostler! Lend us a football!
  Whoop ho! Enow, enow, enow, enow!

[*Exeunt Vices and Mankind*]

45

Mercy. My mind is dispersed, my body trembleth as the aspen
  leaf;
The tears should trickle down by my cheeks, were not your
  reverence.   740
It were to me solace, the cruel visitation of death.
Without rude behaviour I cannot express this inconvenience.
Weeping, sything, and sobbing were my sufficience;
All natural nutriment to me as caren is odible.
My inward affliction yieldeth me tedious unto your presence;
I cannot bear it evenly that Mankind is so flexible.
Man unkind, wherever thou be! For all this world was not
  apprehensible
To discharge thine original offence, thraldom, and captivity,
Till God's own well-beloved son was obedient and passible.
Every drop of his blood was shed to purge thine iniquity.   750
I discommend and disallow thine often mutability.
To every creature thou art dispectuous and odible.
Why art thou so uncurtess, so inconsiderate? Alas, woe is me!
As the fane that turneth with the wind, so thou art convertible.
In trust is treason; thy promise is not credible;
Thy perversiose ingratitude I cannot rehearse.
To God and to all the holy court of heaven thou art despectible
As a noble versifier maketh mention in this verse:
'Lex et natura, Christus et omnia jura
Damnant ingratum, lugent eum fore natum'.   760
Oh good Lady and Mother of mercy, have pity and
  compassion
Of the wretchedness of Mankind that is so wanton and so
Let mercy exceed justice, dear Mother, admit this   frail!
  supplication,
Equity to be laid unparty and mercy to prevail.
Too sensual living is reprovable that is nowadays,
As by the comprehense of this matter it may be specified.
New Guise, Nowadays, Naught with their allectuous ways
They have perverted Mankind, my sweet son, I have well
  espied.
Ah, with these cursed caitiffs, and I may, he shall not long
  endure;
I, Mercy, his father ghostly, will proceed forth and do my
  property.   770
Lady, help! This manner of living is a detestable pleasure:

Vanitas vanitatum, all is but a vanity.
Mercy shall never be convict of his uncurtess condition.
With weeping tears by night and by day I will go and never
Shall I not find him? Yes, I hope. Now God be my   cease.
   protection!
My predilect son, where be ye? Mankind, ubi es?

[Exit Mercy. Enter the Vices]

Mis. My prepotent father, when ye sup, sup out your mess!
   Ye are all to-gloried in your terms; ye make many a lesse.
   Will ye hear? He crieth ever 'Mankind, ubi es?'
New. Hic hic, hic hic, hic hic, hic hic!   780
   That is to say, here here here! Nigh dead in the creek;
   If ye will have him, go and seek, seek, seek:
   Seek not overlong, for losing of your mind!
Now. If ye will have Mankind, how domine domine dominus!
   Ye must speak to the shrive for a cape corpus,
   Else ye must be fain to return with non est inventus.
   How say ye, sir? My bolt is shot.
Naught. I am doing of my needings; beware how ye shot!
   Fie fie fie! I have foul arrayed my fote.
   Be wise for shooting with your tackles, for God wot   790
   My foot is foully overshot.
Mis. A parliament, a parliament! Come forth Naught, behind.
   A council belive! I am afeared Mercy will him find.
   How say ye, and what say ye? How shall we do with
     Mankind?
New. Tish, a fly's wing! Will ye do well?
   He weeneth Mercy were hung for stealing of a mare.
   Mischief, go say to him that Mercy seeketh everywhere.
   He will hung himself, I undertake, for fear.
Mis. I assent thereto; it is wittily said and well.
Now. Whip it in thy coat; anon it were done.   800
   Now Saint Gabriel's mother save the clothes of thy shon!
   All the books in the world, if they had be undone,
   Could not a counselled us bett.

Hic exit Mischief.

Mis. How, Mankind! Come and speak with Mercy, he is here
Man. A rope, a rope, a rope! I am not worthy.   fast by.
Mis. Anon, anon, anon! I have it here ready,
   With a tree also that I have get.

Hold the tree, Nowadays, Naught! Take heed and be wise!

[Enter Mischief with Mankind]

New. Lo, Mankind, do as I do; this is thy new guise;
Give the rope just to thy neck; this is mine avise.   810

[Enter Mercy]

Mis. Help thyself, Naught! Lo, Mercy is here!
He scareth us with a baleis; we may no longer tarry.
New. Queck, queck, queck! Alas my throat! I beshrew you,
      marry!
Ah, Mercy, Christ's copped curse go with you and Saint
Alas, my weasant! Ye were somewhat too near.   Davy!

Exiant.

Mercy. Arise, my precious redempt son! Ye be to me full dear.
He is so timorous, me seemeth his vital spirit doth expire.
Man. Alas, I have be so bestially disposed I dare not appear;
To see your solacious face I am not worthy to desire.
Mercy. Your criminous complaint woundeth my heart as a
      lance.   820
Dispose yourself meekly to ask mercy, and I will assent.
Yield me neither gold nor treasure, but your humble
      obeisance,
The voluntary subjection of your heart, and I am content.
Man. What, ask mercy yet once again? Alas, it were a wild
      petition,
Ever to offend and ever to ask mercy, it is a puerility.
It is so abominable to rehearse my iterate transgression,
I am not worthy to have mercy by no possibility.
Mercy. Oh, Mankind, my singler solace, this is a lamentable
      excuse.
The dolourous tears of my heart, how they begin to amount!
Oh pierced Jesu, help thou this sinful sinner to reduce!   830
'Nam hec est mutacio dextre Excelsi; vertit impios et non
      sunt.'
Arise and ask Mercy, Mankind, and be associate to me;
Thy death shall be my heaviness; alas, 'tis pity it should be
      thus.
Thy obstinacy will exclude thee fro the glorious perpetuity;
Yet for my love ope thy lips and say 'Miserere mei, Deus!'

48

Man. The egall justice of God will not permit such a sinful wretch
To be revived and restored again; it were impossible.
Mercy. The justice of God will as I will, as himself doth precise:
Nolo mortem peccatoris inquit, if he will be reducible.
Man. Then mercy, good Mercy! What is a man without mercy?   840
Little is our part of paradise where mercy ne were.
Good Mercy, excuse the inevitable objection of my ghostly enmy.
The proverb saith 'The truth trieth the self'. Alas, I have much care.
Mercy. God will not make you privy unto his last Judgment.
Justice and Equity shall be fortified, I will not deny.
Troth may not so cruelly proceed in his strait argument
But that Mercy shall rule the matter without controversy.
Arise now and go with me in this deambulatory.
Incline your capacity; my doctrine is convenient.
Sin not in hope of mercy; that is a crime notary;   850
To trust overmuch in a prince it is not expedient:
In hope when ye sin ye think to have mercy, beware of that aventure.
The good Lord said to the lecherous woman of Canaan,
The Holy Gospel is the authority as we read in Scripture,
'Vade et iam amplius noli peccare.'
Christ preserved this sinful woman taken in avowtry;
He said to her these words, 'Go and sin no more.'
So to you, go and sin no more. Beware of vain confidence of mercy;
Offend not a prince on trust of his favour, as I said before.
If ye feel yourself trapped in the snare of your ghostly enmy,   860
Ask mercy anon; beware of the continuance.
While a wound is fresh it is proved curable by surgery,
That if it proceed overlong, it is cause of great grievance.
Man. To ask mercy and to have, this is a liberal possession.
Shall this expeditious petition ever be allowed, as ye have insight?
Mercy. In this present life, mercy is plenty till death maketh his division,
But when ye be go, usque ad minimum quadrantem ye shall reckon your right.

Ask Mercy and have, while the body with the soul hath his
    annexion;
If ye tarry till your decease, ye may hap of your desire to
    miss.
Be repentant here, trust not the hour of death; think on this
    lesson: 870
'Ecce nunc tempus acceptabile, ecce nunc dies salutis.'
All the virtue in the world if ye might comprehend,
Your merits were not premiable to the bliss above,
Not to the least joy of heaven, of your proper effort to
    ascend.
With mercy ye may; I tell you no fable, Scripture doth
    prove.
Man. Oh Mercy, my suavious solace and singular recreatory,
My predilect special, ye are worthy to have my love;
For without desert and means supplicatory
Ye be compatient to my inexcusable reprove.
Ah, it swimmeth my heart to think how unwisely I have
    wrought.   880
Titivillus, that goeth invisible, hung his net before my eye
And by his fantastical visions seditiously sought;
To New Guise, Nowadays, Naught, caused me to obey.
Mercy. Mankind, ye were oblivious of my doctrine monitory.
I said before, Titivillus would assay you a brunt.
Beware fro henceforth of his fables delusory.
The proverb saith, 'jacula prestita minus ledunt.'
Ye have three adversaries, and he is master of hem all:
That is to say, the Devil, the World, the Flesh and the Fell.
The New Guise, Nowadays, Naught, the World we may
    hem call;   .   890
And properly Titivillus signifieth the fiend of Hell;
The Flesh, that is the unclean concupiscence of your body.
These be your three ghostly enmies, in whom ye have put
    your confidence;
They brought you to Mischief to conclude your temporal
    glory,
As it hath be showed before this worshipful audience.
Remember how ready I was to help you; fro such I was not
    dangerous;
Wherefore, good son, abstain fro sin evermore after this.
Ye may both save and spill your soul that is so precious.

50

Libere velle, libere nolle, God may not deny, iwis.
Beware of Titivillus with his net and of all enmies' will,   900
Of your sinful delectation that grieveth your ghostly
    substance.
Your body is your enmy; let him not have his will.
Take your leave when ye will. God send you good
    perseverance!
Man. Sith I shall depart, bless me, father, here then I go.
God send us all plenty of his great mercy.
Mercy. Dominus custodit te ab omni malo
In nomine Patris et Filii et Spiritus Sancti. Amen!

Hic exit Mankind.

Worshipful sovereigns, I have do my property:
Mankind is delivered by my favoural patrociny.
God preserve him fro all wicked captivity   910
And send him grace his sensual conditions to mortify.
Now for His love that for us received his humanity,
Search your conditions with due examination:
Think and remember the world is but a vanity,
As it is proved daily by divers transmutation.
Mankind is wretched, he hath sufficient prove;
Therefore God grant you all per suam misericordiam
That ye may be playferes with the angels above,
And have to your portion vitam eternam. Amen!

FINIS

A play of loue,
A newe and a

mery enterlude concernyng plea-

sure and payne in loue,

made by Iohn

Heywood.

The players

names.

A man a louer not beloued.

A woman beloued not louyng.

A man a louer and beloued.

The vyse nother louer nor beloued.

A PLAY OF LOVE

[*Lover-not-loved enters.*]

Lover-not-loved

Lo, sir, whoso that looketh here for courtesy
And seeth me seem as one pretending none,
But as unthought upon thus suddenly
Approacheth the mids among you everychon,
And of you all saith naught to anyone,
May think me rude, perceiving of what sort
Ye seem to be, and of what stately port.

But I beseech you in most humble wise
To omit displeasure and pardon me;
My manner is to muse and to devise   10
So that some time myself may carry me
Myself knoweth not where, and I assure ye
So hath myself done now, for our Lord wot
Where I am, or what ye be, I know not,

Or whence I came, or whither I shall,
All this in manner as unknowen to me;
But even as Fortune guideth my foot to fall
So wander I, yet wheresoever I be
And whom or how many soever I see,
As one person to me is everychon,   20
So every place to me but as one.

And for that one person every place seek I,
Which one once found, I find of all the rest
Not one missing, and in the contrary
That one absent, though that there were here pressed
All the creatures living, most and lest,
Yet lacking her, I should and ever shall
Be as alone, since she to me is all.

And alone is she without comparison,
Concerning the gifts given by nature.   30
In favour, fairness, and port as of person
No life beareth the like of that creature,

53

Nor no tongue can attain to put in ure
Her to describe, for how can words express
That thing, the full whereof no thought can guess?

And as it is a thing inestimable
To make report of her beauty fully,
So is my love toward her unable
To be reported, as who saith rightly,
For my full service and love to that lady   40
Is given under such abundant fashion
That no tongue thereof can make right relation.

Wherein I suppose this well supposed
Unto you all, that since she perceiving
As much of my love as can be disclosed,
Even of very right in recompensing
She ought for my love again to be loving;
For what more right to grant when love love requireth,
Than love for love, when love naught else desireth?

But even as far worse as otherwise than so   50
Stand I in case, in manner desperate;
No time can time my suit to ease my woe,
Before noon too early and all times else too late:
Thus time out of time mistimeth my rate,
For time to bring time to hope of any grace
That time timeth no time in any time or place.

Whereby till time have time so far extinct,
That death may determine my life thus deadly
No time can I rest. Alas, I am so linked
To griefs both so great and also many   60
That by the same I say, and will verify,
Of all pains the most incomparable pain
Is to be a lover not loved again.

The woman beloved not loving entreth.

Loved-not-loving
Sir, as touching those words of comparison
Which ye have said and would seem to verify,
If it may please you to stand thereupon
Hearing and answering me patiently,
I doubt not by the same incontinently

Yourself to see, by words that shall ensue,
The contrary of your words verified for true.   70

Lover-not-loved.
  Fair lady, pleaseth it you to repair near
  And in this cause to show cause reasonable
  Whereby cause of reformation may appear,
  Of reason I must and will be reformable.
Loved-not-loving.
  Well, since ye pretend to be conformable
  To reason, in avoiding circumstance,
  Briefly by reason I shall the truth advance.

  Ye be a lover no whit loved again,
  And I am loved of whom I love nothing:
  Then standeth our question between these twain   80
  Of loving not loved, or loved not loving,
  Which is the case most painful in suffering;
  Whereto I say that the most pain doth move
  To those beloved of whom they cannot love.

Lover-not-loved.
  Those words approved, lo, might make a change
  Of mine opinion, but verily
  The case as ye put it I think more strange
  Than true, for though the beloved party
  Cannot love again, yet possibly
  Can I not think, nor I think never shall   90
  That to be loved can be any pain at all.

Loved-not-loving.
  That reason perceived, and received for troth
  From proper comparison, should clear confound me;
  Between pain and no pain, no such comparison groweth.
  Then, or I can on comparison ground me,
  To prove my case painful ye have first bound me;
  To which, since ye drive me by your denial,
  Mark what ensueth before further trial.

  I say I am loved of a certain man
  Whom for no suit I can favour again,   100
  And that have I told him since his suit began
  A thousand times, but every time in vain;

For never ceaseth his tongue to complain,
And ever one tale which I never can flee,
For ever in manner where I am is he.

Now if you to hear one thing everywhere
Contrary to your appetite should be led,
Were it but a mouse, lo, should peep in your ear
Or alway to harp on a crust of bread,
How could you like such harping at your head? 110
Lover-not-loved. Somewhat displeasant it were, I not deny.
Loved-not-loving. Then somewhat painful as well said, say I:

Displeasure and pain be things jointly annexed,
For as it is displeasant in pain to be,
So it is painful in displeasure to be vexed.
Thus by displeasure in pain ye confess me,
Whereby since ye part of my pain do see
In my further pain I shall now declare
That pain by which with your pain I compare.

Small were the quantity of my painful smart 120
If his jangling pierced no further than mine ears,
But thorough mine ears directly to mine heart
Pierceth his words, even like as many spears;
By which I have spent so many and such tears
That were they all red as they be all white,
The blood of my heart had be gone or this quite.

And almost in case as though it were gone
Am I, except his suit take end shortly;
For it doth like me even like as one
Should offer me service most humbly 130
With an axe in his hand, continually
Beseeching me gently that this might be sped
To grant him my good will to strike off my head.

I allege for general this one similitude,
Avoiding rehearsal of pains particular,
To abbreviate the time, and to exclude
Surplusage of words in this our matter;
By which example if ye consider
Rightly my case, at leastwise ye may see
My pain as painful as your pain can be. 140

And yet for shorter end, put case that your pain
Were oft times more sharp and sore in degree
Than mine is at any time, yet will I prove plain
My pain at length sufficient to match ye;
Which proof to be true yourself shall agree,
If your affection in that I shall recite
May suffer your reason to understand right.

You stand in pleasure, having your love in sight,
And in her absence hope of sight again
Keepeth most times possession of some delight;   150
Thus have you oft times some way ease of pain,
And I never no way, for when I do remain
In his presence, in deadly pain I sojourn,
And absent, half dead in fear of his return.

Since presence nor absence absenteth my pain
But alway the same to me is present,
And that by presence and hope of presence again
There doth appear much of your time spent
Out of pain, me think this consequent:
That my pain may well by mean of the length   160
Compare with your shorter pain of more strength.

Lover-not-loved.
Mistress, if your long pain be no stronger
Than is your long reason against my short pain,
Ye lack no likelihood to live much longer
Than he that would strike off your head so fain.
Yet lest ye would note me your words to disdain,
I am content to agree for a season
To grant and enlarge your latter reason.

Admit by her presence half my time pleasant,
And all your time as painful as in case can be,   170
Yet your pain to be most reason will not grant;
And for example, I put case that ye
Stood in cold water all a day to the knee,
And I half the same day to mid leg in the fire:
Would ye change places with me for the drier?

Loved-not-loving.
Nay, that would I not, be ye assured.

57

Forsooth, and my pain above yours is as ill
As fire above water thus to be endured.
Came my pain but at times and yours continue still,
Yet should mine many ways, to whom can skill,   180
Show yours, in comparison between the twain,
Scantly able for a shadow to my pain.

Felt ye but one pang such as I feel many:
One pang of despair, or one pang of desire,
One pang of one displeasant look of her eye,
One pang of one word of her mouth, as in ire
Or in restraint of her love which I require,
One pang of all these felt once in all your life
Should quail your opinion and quench all our strife.

Which pangs I say, admitted short as ye list,   190
And all my time beside pleasant as ye please,
Yet could not the shortness the sharpness so resist.
The piercing of my heart in the least of all these
But much it overmatcheth all your disease,
For no whit in effect is your case displeasant
But to deny a thing which ye list not to grant,

Or to hear a suitor by daily petition,
In humble manner as wit can devise,
Require a thing, so standing in condition
As no portion of all his enterprise   200
Without your consent can speed in any wise.
This suit thus attempted never so long,
Doubt ye no death till your pain be more strong.

Now since in this matter between us disputed,
Mine admittance of your words notwithstanding,
I have thus fully your part confuted,
What can ye say now I come to denying
Your principal, granted in my foresaying?
Which was this, by the presence of my lady
I granted you half my time spent pleasantly.   210

Although mine affection leadeth me to consent
That her seld presence is my relief only,
Yet, as in reason appeareth, all my torment

Bred by her presence, and mark this cause why:
Before I saw her I felt no malady,
And since I saw her I never was free
From twain the greatest pains that in love be.

Desire is the first upon my first sight,
And despair the next upon my first suit;
For upon her first answer hope was put to flight,   220
And never came since in place to dispute.
How bringeth then her presence to me any fruit?
For hopeless and helpless, in flames of desire
And drops of despair I smoulder in fire.

These twain being endless since they began,
And both by the presence of her wholly
Begun and continued, I wonder if ye can
Speak any word more, but yield immediately;
For had I no mo pains but these, yet clearly
A thousand times more is my grief in these twain   230
Than yours in all the case by which ye complain.

Loved-not-loving.
That is as ye say, but not as I suppose,
Nor as the truth is, which yourself might see
By reasons that I could and would disclose,
Saving that I see such partiality
On your part, that we shall never agree,
Unless ye will admit some man indifferent
Indifferently to hear us, and so give judgement.

Lover-not-loved.
Agree, for though the knowledge of all my pain
Ease my pain no whit, yet shall it declare   240
Great cause of abashment in you, to complain
In counterfeit pains with my pain to compare:
But here is no judge meet, we must seek elsewhere.
Loved-not-loving.
I hold me content the same to condescend,
Please it you to set forth and I shall attend.

> *Here they go both out and the Lover beloved
> entreth with a song.*

By common experience who can deny
Impossibility for man to show
His inward intent, but by signs outwardly,
As writing, speech, or countenance; whereby doth grow
Outward perceiving inwardly to know   250
Of every secrecy in man's breast wrought,
Fro man unto man the effect of each thought.

These things well weighed in many things show need
In our outward signs to show us, so that plain
According to our thoughts, words, and signs proceed;
For in outward signs where men are seen to feign
What credence in man to man may remain?
Man's inward mind with outward signs to fable,
May soon be more common than commendable.

Much are we lovers then to be commended,   260
For love his appearance dissembleth in no wise,
But as the heart feeleth, like signs alway pretended.
Who feign in appearance are love's mortal enmies;
As in despair of speed who that can mirth devise,
Or having grant of grace can show them as mourners,
Such be no lovers, but even very scorners.

The true lover's heart that cannot obtain
Is so tormented, that all the body
Is evermore so compelled to complain,
That sooner may the sufferer hide the fury   270
Of a fervent fever, than of that malady
By any power human he possibly may
Hide the least pain of a thousand I dare say.

And he who in loving hath lot to such luck
That love for love of his love be found,
Shall be of power even as easily to pluck
The moon in a moment with a finger to ground,
As of his joy to enclose the rebound,
But that the reflection thereof from his heart
To his beholders shall shine in each part.   280

Thus be a lover in joy or in care,
Although will and wit his estate would hide,

Yet shall his semblance as a dial declare
How the clock goeth, which may be well applied
In abridgement of circumstance for a guide,
To lead you in few words by my behaviour
To know me in grace of my lady's favour.

For being a lover, as I am indeed,
And thereto disposed thus pleasantly,
Is a plain appearance of my such speed   290
As I in love could wish, and undoubtedly
My love is requited so lovingly,
That in everything that may delight my mind
My wit can not wish it so well as I find.

Which thing at full considered, I suppose
That all the whole world must agree in one voice,
I being beloved, as I now disclose,
Of one being chief of all the whole choice,
Must have incomparable cause to rejoice;
For the highest pleasure that man may obtain   300
Is to be a lover beloved again.

Nother-Lover-nor-loved entreth.

No-lover-nor-loved. Now, god you good even, Master Woodcock.
Lover-loved. Cometh of rudeness or lewdness that mock?
No-lover-nor-loved.
    Come whereof it shall, ye come of such stock
    That god you good even, Master Woodcock.
Lover-loved. This losel belike hath lost his wit!
No-lover-nor-loved.
    Nay, nay, Master Woodcock, not a whit;
    I have known you for a woodcock or this,
    Or else like a woodcock I take you amiss;
    But though for a woodcock ye deny the same,   310
    Yet shall your wit witness you meet for that name.
Lover-loved. How so?
No-lover-nor-loved. Thus lo:
    I do perceive, by your former process,
    That ye be a lover, whereto ye confess
    Yourself beloved in as loving wise
    As by wit and will ye can wish to devise;
    Concluding therein determinately,

61

That of all pleasures pleasant to the body,
The highest pleasure that man may obtain   320
Is to be a lover beloved again:
In which conclusion, before all this flock,
I shall prove you plain as wise as a woodcock.
Lover-loved.
And methink this woodcock is turned on thy side;
Contrary to court'sy and reason to use,
Thus rudely to rail or any word be tried
In proof of thy part, whereby I do refuse
To answer the same. Thou canst not excuse
Thy folly in this, but if thou wilt say aught,
Assay to say better, for this saying is naught.   330
No-lover-nor-loved.
Well, since it is so that ye be discontent
To be called fool or further matter be spent,
Will ye give me leave to call ye fool anon,
When yourself perceiveth that I have proved you one?
Lover-loved. Yea, by my soul, and will take it in good worth.
No-lover-nor-loved.
Now by my father's soul, then will we even forth.
That part rehearsed of your saying or this
Of all our debate the only cause is;
For where ye afore have fastly affirmed
That such as be lovers again beloved   340
Stand in most pleasure that to man may move,
That tale to be false truth shall truly prove.
Lover-loved. What folk above those live more pleasantly?
No-lover-nor-loved. What folk? Marry, even such folk as am I.
Lover-loved. Being no lover, what man may ye be?
No-lover-nor-loved.
No lover? No, by god I warrant ye.
I am no lover in such manner meant
As doth appear in this purpose present,
For as touching women, go where I shall
I am at one point with women all.   350
The smoothest, the smirkest, the smallest,
The truest, the trimmest, the tallest,
The wisest, the wiliest, the wildest,
The merriest, the mannerliest, the mildest,
The strangest, the straightest, the strongest,

62

The lustiest, the least, or the longest,
The rashest, the ruddiest, the roundest,
The sagest, the sallowest, the soundest,
The coyest, the curstest, the coldest,
The busiest, the brightest, the boldest,   360
The thankfullest, the thinnest, the thickest,
The saintliest, the sourest, the sickest;
Take these with all the rest, and of everychon
So God be my help I love never one.
Lover-loved.
Then I beseech thee this one thing tell me,
How many women thinkest thou doth love thee?
No-lover-nor-loved.
Sir as I be saved, by aught I can prove
I am beloved even like as I love.
Lover-loved.
Then as appeareth by those words rehearsed,
Thou art nother lover nor beloved.   370
No-lover-nor-loved. Nother lover nor beloved, that is even true.
Lover-loved.
Since that is true, I marvel what can ensue
For proof of thy part, in that thou madest avaunt
Of both our estates to prove thine most pleasant.
No-lover-nor-loved.
My part for most pleasant may soon be guessed
By my continual quieted rest.
Lover-loved. Being no lover who may quiet be?
No-lover-nor-loved.
Nay, being a lover what man is he
That is quiet?
Lover-loved. Marry I.   380
No-lover-nor-loved. Marry ye lie.
Lover-loved.
What, patience, my friend, ye are too hasty;
If ye will patiently mark what I shall say,
Yourself shall perceive me in quiet alway.
No-lover-nor-loved.
Say what thou will, and I therein protest
To believe no word thou sayest most nor lest.
Lover-loved.
Then we twain shall talk both in vain I see,

63

Except our matter awarded may be
By judgement of some indifferent hearer.

No-lover-nor-loved.

Marry, go thou and be an inquirer,   390
And if thou canst bring one anything likely,
He shall be admitted for my part quickly.

Lover-loved.

Now by the good God I grant to agree,
For be thou assured, it scorneth me
That thou shouldest compare in pleasure to be
Like me, and surely I promise thee
One way or other I will find redress.

No-lover-nor-loved.

Find the best and next way thy wit can guess,
And except your nobs for malice do need ye
Make brief return: a fellowship speed ye.   400

The Lover loved goeth out.

No-lover-nor-loved.

My marvel is no more than my care is small,
What knave this fool shall bring being not partial.
And yet be he false and a foolish knave too,
So that it be not too much ado
To bring a daw to hear and speak right,
I force for no man the worth of a mite;
And since my doubt is so small in good speed
What should my study be more than my need?
Till time I perceive this woodcock coming,
My part hereof should pass even in mumming,   410
Saving for pastime, since I consider
He being a lover and all his matter
To depend on love, and contrary I
No lover, by which all such standing by
As favour my part, may fear me too weak
Against the loving of this lover to speak,
I shall for your comfort declare such a story
As shall perfectly plant in your memory
That I have knowledge in lovers' laws,
As deep as some dozen of those doting daws;   420
Which told, all ye whose fancies stick near me
Shall know it causeless in this case to fear me;

For though as I show I am no lover now,
Nor never have been, yet shall I show you
How that I once chanced to take in hand
To feign myself a lover, ye shall understand,
Toward such a sweeting, as by sweet Saint Saviour,
I know not the like in fashion and favour:
And to begin
At setting in,
First was her skin   430
White, smooth, and thin,
And every vein
So blue seen plain,
Her golden hair
To see her wear,
Her wearing gear—
Alas I fear
To tell all to you;
I shall undo you.   440
Her eye so rolling,
Each heart controlling,
Her nose not long,
Nor stood not wrong,
Her finger tips
So clean she clips;
Her rosy lips
Her cheeks gossips;
So fair so ruddy,
It asketh study;   450
The whole to tell
It did excell,
It was so made
That even the shade
At every glade
Would hearts invade;
The paps so small,
And round withal,
The waist not mickle
But it was tickle;   460
The thigh, the knee,
As they should be;
But such a leg

A lover would beg
To set eye on,
But it is gone.
Then sight of the fote
Rift hearts to the rote,
And last of all, Saint Catherine's wheel
Was never so round as was her heel.   470
Assault her heart, and who could win it?
As for her heel, no hold in it.
Yet over that her beauty was so much,
In pleasant qualities her graces were such
For dalliant pastance, pass where she should,
No greater difference between lead and gold
Than between the rest and her, and such a wit
That no wight I ween might match her in it.
If she had not wit to set wise men to school,
Then shall my tale prove me a stark fool   480
But in this matter to make you meet to guess,
Ye shall understand that I with this mistress
Fell late acquainted, and for love no whit,
But for my pleasure to approve my wit.
How I could love to this tricker dissimble,
Who in dissimuling was perfect and nimble;
For where or when she list to give a mock
She could and would do it beyond the nock;
Wherein I thought that if I triced her
I should thereby like my wit the better,   490
And if she chanced to trip or trice me,
It should to learn wit a good lesson be.
Thus for my pastime, I did determine
To mock or be mocked of this mocking vermin,
For which her presence I did first obtain,
And that obtained, forthwith fell we twain
In great acquaintance and made as good cheer
As we had been acquainted twenty year,
And I through fair flattering behaviour
Seemed anon so deep in her favour,   500
That though the time then so far passed was
That time required us asunder to pass,
Yet could I no passport get of my sweeting
Till I was full wooed for the next day's meeting,

66

For surance whereof I must as she bade
Give her in gage best jewel I there had;
And after much mirth as our wits could devise,
We parted, and I the next morn did arise
In time not too timely—such time as I could
(I allow no love where sleep is not allowed).   510
I was, or I entered this journey vowed,
Decked very cleanly but not very proud,
But trim must I be, for slovenly lubbers
Have, ye wot well, no place among lovers.
But I thus decked, at all points point device,
At door where this trull was I was at a trice,
Whereat I knocked her presence to win,
Wherewith it was opened and I was let in;
And at my first coming my minion seemed
Very merry, but anon she misdeemed   520
That I was not merrily disposed,
And so might she think, for I disclosed
No word nor look, but such as showed as sadly
As I indeed inwardly thought madly.
And so must I show, for lovers be in rate,
Sometimes merry, but most times passionate.
In giving thanks to her of overnight
We set us down, an heavy couple in sight,
And therewithal I set a sigh, such one
As made the form shake which we both sat on,   530
Whereupon she without more words spoken
Fell in weeping as her heart should have broken,
And I in secret laughing, so heartily
That from mine eyes came water plenteously.
Anon I turned with look sadly, that she
My weeping as watery as hers might see,
Which done, these words anon to me she spake:
'Alas, dear heart, what wight might undertake
To show one so sad as you this morning,
Being so merry as you last evening?   540
I so far then the merrier for you,
And without desert thus far the sadder now.'
'The self thing,' quoth I, 'which made me then glad,
The self same is thing that maketh me now sad:
The love that I owe you is original

67

Ground of my late joy and present pain all,
And by this mean, love is evermore lad
Between two angels, one good and one bad,
Hope and Dread, which two be alway at strife
Which one of them both with love shall rule most rife.   550
And Hope, that good angel, first part of last night
Drew Dread, that bad angel, out of place quite.
Hope swore I should straight have your love at ones,
And Dread, this bad angel, swore blood and bones
That if I won your love all in one hour,
I should lose it all again in three or four;
Wherein this good angel hath lost the mast'ry,
And I by this bad angel won this agony,
And be ye sure I stand now in such case,
That if I lack your continued grace,   560
In heaven, hell, or earth, there is not that he
(Save only God) that knoweth what shall come on me.
I love not in rate all the common flock,
I am no feigner, nor I cannot mock,
Wherefore I beseech you that your reward
May witness that ye do my truth regard.'
'Sir as touching mocking,' quoth she, 'I am sure
Ye be too wise to put that here in ure,
For nother give I cause why ye so should do,
Nor naught could ye win that way worth an old shoe,   570
For who so that mocketh shall surely stir
This old proverb, 'moccum moccabitur.'
But as for you, I think myself assured
That very love hath you hither allured,
For which,' quoth she, 'let Hope hop up again
And vanquish Dread, so that it be in vain
To dread or to doubt; but I in everything
As cause giveth cause will be your own darling.'
'Sweetheart,' quoth I, 'after stormy cold smarts,
Warm words in warm lovers bring lovers warm hearts,   580
And so have your words warmed my heart even now,
That dreadless and doubtless now must I love you.'
Anon there was 'I love you' and 'I love you'
(Lovely we lovers love each other)
'I love you' and 'I for love love you';
My lovely loving loved brother,

Love me, love thee, love we, love he, love she,
Deeper love apparent in no twain can be.
Quite over the ears in love, and felt no ground;
Had not swimming holp, in love I had been drowned;   590
But I swam by the shore the vantage to keep,
To mock her in love, seeming to swim more deep.
Thus continued we day by day,
Till time that a moneth was passed away,
In all the which time such a weight she took
That by no mean I might once set one look
Upon any woman in company,
But straightway she set the finger in the eye,
And by that same aptness in jealousy
I thought sure she loved me perfectly;   600
And I, to show myself in like loving,
Dissimuled like cheer in all her like looking.
By this and other like things then in hand
I gave her mocks, methought, above a thousand;
Whereby I thought her own tale like a burr
Stuck to her own back, moccum moccabitur.
And upon this I fell in devising
To bring to end this idle disguising,
Whereupon suddenly I stole away,
And when I had been absent half a day   610
My heart misgave me, by God that bought me,
That if she missed me where I thought she sought me,
She sure would be mad by love that she ought me,
Wherein not love, but pity so wrought me
That to return anon I bethought me;
And so returned till chance had brought me
To her chamber door, and hard I knocked.
'Knock soft,' quoth one who the same unlocked—
An ancient wise woman who was never
From this said sweeting, but about her ever—   620
'Mother,' quoth I, 'how doth my dear darling?'
'Dead, wretch,' cried she, 'even by thine absenting.'
And without mo words the door to her she shit,
I standing without half out of my wit,
In that this woman should die in my fault;
But since I could in there by none assault,
To her chamber window I got about,

To see at the least way the corse laid out,
And there looking in, by God's blessed mother,
I saw her naked abed with another,   630
And with her bed-fellow laughed me to scorn
As merrily as ever she laughed beforn!
The which when I saw, and then remembered
The terrible words that Mother B rendered,
And also bethought me of everything
Showed in this woman true love betokening,
Myself to see served thus prettily
To myself I laughed even heartily,
With myself considering to have had like speed
If myself had been a lover indeed.   640
But now to make some matter whereby
I may take my leave of my love honestly:
'Sweetheart,' quoth I, 'ye take too much upon ye.'
'No more than becomes me, know thou well,' quoth she.
'But thou hast taken too much upon thee,
In taking that thou took in hand to mock me,
Wherein from beginning I have seen thee jet
Like as a fool might have jetted in a net,
Believing himself, save of himself only,
To be perceived of no living body.   650
But well saw I thine intent at beginning
Was to bestow a mock on me at ending;
When thou laughedest, dissimuling a weeping heart,
Then I with weeping eyes played even the like part,
Wherewith I brought in moccum moccabitur,
And yet thou, being a long-snouted cur,
Could no whit smell that all my meaning was
To give mock for mock, as now is come to pass,
Which now thus passed, if thy wit be handsome,
May defend thee from mocks in time to come,   660
By clapping fast to thy snout every day
Moccum moccabitur for a nosegay.'
Wherewith she start up and shut her window to;
Which done, I had no more to say nor do
But think myself or any man else a fool
In mocks or wiles to set women to school.
But now to purpose wherefore I began.
Although I were made a fool by this woman

70

Concerning mocking, yet doth this tale approve
That I am well seen in the art of love,   670
For I intending no love but to mock,
Yet could no lover of all the whole flock
Circumstance of love disclose more nor better
Than did I, the substance being no greater;
And by this tale afore ye, all may see
Although a lover as well loved be
As love can devise him for pleasant speed,
Yet two displeasures, jealousy and dread,
Is mixed with love, whereby love is a drink meet
To give babes for worms, for it drinketh bittersweet.   680
And as for this babe our lover, in whose head
By a frantic worm his opinion is bred,
After one draught of this medicine ministered
Into his brain, by my brain appointed,
Reason shall so temper his opinion
That he shall see it not worth an onion,
And if he have any other thing to lay
I have to convince him every way.
And since my part now doth thus well appear,
Be ye my parteners now, all of good cheer—   690
But silence every man upon a pain,
For Master Woodcock is now come again.

The Lover loved entreth.

Lover-loved.
    The old saying saith, he that seeketh shall find,
    Which after long seeking true have I found;
    But for such a finding myself to bind
    To such a seeking as I was now bound,
    I would rather seek to lose twenty pound.
    Howbeit, I have sought so far to my pain,
    That at the last I have found and brought twain.

The Lover not loved, and Loved not loving entreth.

No-lover-nor-loved. Come they a horseback?   700
Lover-loved.   Nay, they come afoot.
    Which thou might see here, but for this great mist.
No-lover-nor-loved.
    By jis, and yet see I, thou blind bald coot,

71

That one of those twain might ride if he list.

Lover-loved. How?

No-lover-nor-loved.

Marry, for he leadeth a nag on his fist.

Mistress ye are welcome, and welcome ye be.

Loved-not-loving. Nay welcome be ye, for we were here before ye.

No-lover-nor-loved.

Ye have been here before me before now,
And now I am here before you,   710
And now I am here behind ye,
And now ye be here behind me,
And now we be here even both together,
And now be we welcome even both hither;
Since now ye find me here, with court'sy I may
Bid you welcome hither as I may say.
But setting this aside, let us set abroach
The matter wherefore ye hither approach,
Wherein I have hope that ye both will be
Good unto me, and especially ye;   720
For I have a mind that every good face
Hath ever some pity of a poor man's case,
Being, as mine is, a matter so right
That a fool may judge it right at first sight.

Lover-not-loved.

Sir, ye may well doubt how my wit will serve,
But my will from right shall never swerve.

Loved-not-loving.

Nor mine, and as ye sue for help to me
Like suit have I to sue for help to ye,
For as much need have I of help as yow.

No-lover-nor-loved. I think well that, dear heart, but tell me how?   730

Loved-not-loving.

The case is this. Ye twain seem in pleasure
And we twain in pain, which pain doth procure
By comparison between him and me
As great a conflict which of us twain be
In greatest pain, as is between ye twain
Which of you twain in most pleasure doth remain;
Wherein we somewhat have here debated,
And both to tell truth so greedily grated
Upon affection each to our own side,

That in conclusion, we must needs provide 740
Some such as would and could be indifferent,
And we both to stand unto that judgement;
Whereupon for lack of a judge in this place
We sought many places, and yet in this case
No man could we meet that meddle will or can,
Till time that we met with this gentleman,
Whom in like errand for like lack of aid
Was driven to desire our judgement, he said.
Lover-loved.
Forsooth it is so, I promising plain
They twain between us twain giving judgement plain, 750
We twain between them twain should judge right again.
No-lover-nor-loved.
That promise to perform I not disdain,
For touching right, as I am a righteous man
I will give you as much right as I can.
Loved-not-loving.
Nothing but right desire I you among,
I willingly will nother give nor take wrong.
No-lover-nor-loved.
Nay in my conscience I think by this book,
Your conscience will take nothing that cometh acrook;
For as in conscience whatever ye do,
Ye nothing do but as ye would be done to. 760
Oh hope of good end, Oh Mary mother!
Mistress, one of us may now help another.
But sir, I pray you some matter declare
Whereby I may know in what grief ye are.
Lover-not-loved.
I am a lover not loved, which plain
Is daily not doleful but my deadly pain.
No-lover-nor-loved. A lover not loved, have ye knit that knot?
Lover-not-loved. Yea forsooth.
No-lover-nor-loved.   Forsooth ye be the more sot.
Now mistress I heartily beseech ye 770
Tell me what manner case your case may be.
Loved-not-loving.
I am beloved not loving, whereby
I am not in pain but in tormentry.
No-lover-nor-loved. Is this your tormentor? God turn him to good!

73

Loved-not-loving.
>Nay, there is another man on me as wood
>As this man on another woman is.

No-lover-nor-loved.
>Ye think them both mad, and so do I by jis
>So mot I thrive; but who that list to mark
>Shall perceive here a pretty piece of wark.
>Let us fall somewhat in these parts to scanning   780
>Loving not loved, loved not loving,
>Loved and loving, not loving nor loved,
>Will ye see these four parts well joined?
>Loving not loved, and loved not loving:
>Those parts can join in no manner reckoning.
>Loving and loved, loved nor lover:
>These parts in joining in like wise differ.
>But in that ye love ye twain joined be,
>And being not loved ye join with me,
>And being no lover with me joineth she,   790
>And being beloved, with her join ye:
>Had I a joiner with me joined jointly,
>We joiners should join joint to joint quickly;
>For first I would part these parts in fleeces,
>And once departed these parted pieces,
>Part and part with part I would so partlike part,
>That each part should part with quiet heart.

Lover-not-loved.
>Sir, since it passeth your power that part to play,
>Let pass, and let us partly now assay
>To bring some part of that purpose to end   800
>For which all parties yet in vain attend.

Loved-not-loving.
>I do desire the same, and that we twain
>May first be heard that I may know my pain.

Lover-loved.
>I grant for my part, by faith of my body—
>Why where the devil is this whoreson noddy?

No-lover-nor-loved.
>I never sit in justice, but evermore
>I use to be shriven a little before,
>And now since that my confession is done
>I will depart and come take penance sone.

When conscience pricketh, conscience must be searched,
    by God,   810
In discharging of conscience or else Gods forbod;
Which maketh me meet when conscience must come in place,
To be a judge in every common case.
But who may like me his avancement avaunt?
Now am I a judge, and never was serjeant,
Which ye regard not much by aught that I see
By any reverence that ye do to me.
Nay, yet I praise women; when great men go by
They crouch to the ground, look here how they lie:
They shall have a beck, by Saint Antony.   820
But alas, good mistress, I cry you mercy
That you are unanswered, but ye may see
Though two tales at once by two ears heard may be,
Yet cannot one mouth two tales at once answer,
Which maketh you tarry. But in your matter,
Since ye by haste in having furthest home,
Would first be sped of that for which ye come,
I grant as he granted your will to fulfil:
You twain to be heard first. Begin when you will.

Lover-not-loved.

As these twain us twain now grant first to break,   830
Since twain to be heard at once cannot speak,
I now desire your grant, that I may open
First tale which now is at point to be spoken
Which I crave no whit my part to avance,
But with the pith to avoid circumstance.

Loved-not-loving.

Speak what and when soever it please you;
Till reason will me, I will not disease you.

Lover-not-loved.

Sirs, other here is a very weak brain,
Or she hath, if any, a very weak pain;
For I put case that my love I her gave,   840
And that for my love her love I did crave,
For which, though I daily sue day by day,
What loss or pain to her if she say nay?

No-lover-nor-loved.

Yes, by Saint Mary, so the case may stand
That some woman had lever take in hand

75

To ride on your errand one hundreth mile,
Than to say nay one paternoster while.
Lover-not-loved.
    If ye on her part any pain define,
Which is the more painful, her pain or mine?
No-lover-nor-loved.
    Your pain is most if she say nay and take it;   850
But if that she say nay and forsake it
Then is her pain a great way the greater.
Loved-not-loving.
    Sir, ye allege this 'nay' in this matter
As though my denial my suitor to love
Were all or the most pain that to me doth move;
Wherein the truth is a contrary plain,
For though too oft speaking one thing be a pain,
Yet is that one word the full of my hoping
To bring his hoping to despair at ending.
Thus is this nay, which ye take my most grief,   860
Though it be painful, yet my most relief;
But my most pain is all another thing
Which, though ye forget or hide by dissimuling,
I partly showed you, but all I could nor can.
But masters, to you; with pain of this man
That pain that I compare is partly this:
I am loved of one whom the truth is
I cannot love, and so it is with me
That from him in manner I never can flee,
And every one word in suit of his part   870
Nips through mine ears and runs through my heart.
His gastfull look so pale that uneath I
Dare for mine ears cast toward him an eye,
And when I do that eye his thought presenteth
Straight to my heart, and thus my pain augmenteth.
One tale so oft, alas, and so importune;
His exclamations sometime on fortune,
Sometime on himself, sometime upon me,
And for that thing that if my death should be
Brought straight in place, except I were content   880
To grant the same, yet could I not assent;
And he seeing this yet ceaseth not to crave—
What death could be worse than this life that I have?

Lover-not-loved.
This tale to purpose purporteth no more,
But sight and hearing complaint of his sore
Is only the grief that ye do sustain.
Alas, tender heart, since ye die in pain,
This pain to perceive by sight and hearing,
How could you live to know our pain by feeling?
Mark well this question and answer as ye can: 890
A man that is hanged or that man's hangman,
Which man of those twain suffereth most pain?
Loved-not-loving. He that is hanged.
No-lover-nor-loved.   By the mass, it is so plain.
Lover-not-loved.
Well said for me, for I am the sufferer,
And ye the hangman understand as it were.
These cases vary in no manner a thing,
Saving this service in this man's hanging
Commonly is done against the hangman's will,
And ye of delightful will your lover kill.   900
Loved-not-loving.
Of delightful will? Nay that is not so,
As ye shall perfectly perceive or we go.
But of those at whose hanging have hangmen by,
How many have ye knowen hang willingly?
No-lover-nor-loved. Nay never one in his life, by'r Lady.
Loved-not-loving.
In this, lo, your case from our case doth vary,
For ye that love where love will take no place,
Your own will is your own leader a plain case;
And not only uncompelled without allure,
But sore against her will your suit ye endure.   910
Now, since your will to love did you procure,
And with that will ye put that love in ure,
And now that will by wit seeth love such pain
As witty will would will love to refrain,
And ye by will that love in each condition
To extinct, may be your own physician,
Except ye be a fool or would make me one,
What saying could set a good ground to sit on
To make any man think your pain thus strong,
Making your own salve your own sore thus long?   920

77

Lover-not-loved.

Mistress, much part of this process purposed
Is matter of truth truly disclosed.
My will without her will brought me in love,
Which will without her will doth make me hove
Upon her grace to see what grace will prove;
But where ye say my will may me remove
As well from her love, as will brought me to it,
That is false: my will cannot will to do it.
My will as far therein outweigheth my power
As a sow of lead outweigheth a saffron flower.   930

Loved-not-loving.

Your will outweigheth your power, then where is your wit?
I marvel that ever ye will speak it.

Lover-loved.

Nay marvel ye mistress thereat no whit,
For as far as this point may stretch in verdit
I am clearly of this man's opinion.

No-lover-nor-loved. And I contrary, with this minion.

Lover-loved. Then be we come to a demurrer in law.

No-lover-nor-loved.

Then be ye come from a woodcock to a daw,
And by God it is no small cunning, brother,
For me to turn one wild fowl to another.   940

Lover-not-loved.

Nay masters, I heartily pray you both,
Banish contention till ye see how this goeth:
I will repeat and answer her tale forthwith,
The pith for your part whereof pretendeth
A proof for your pain to be more than mine,
In that my will not only did me incline
To the same, but in the same by the same will
I willingly will to continue still,
And as will brought me and keepeth in this bay,
When I will, ye say, will will bring me away;   950
Concluding thereby, that if my pain were
As great as yours, that I should surely bear
As great and good will to flee my love thus meant,
As do ye your suiter's presence to absent.

Loved-not-loving.

This tale showeth my tale perceived every dell.

78

Lover-not-loved.
    Then for entry to answer it as well,
    Answer this: put case ye as deeply now
    Did love your lover as he doth love yow,
    Should not that loving, suppose ye, redress
    That pain which lack of loving doth possess?   960
Loved-not-loving. Yes.
Lover-not-loved.
    Since love given to him giveth yourself ease, than
    Except ye love pain, why love ye not this man?
Loved-not-loving.
    Love him? Nay, as I said, must I straight choose
    To love him or else my head here to lose,
    I know well I could not my life to save
    With loving will grant him my love to have.
Lover-not-loved.
    I think ye speak truly, for will will not be
    Forced in love, wherefore the same to ye:
    Since this is to you such difficulty,   970
    Why not a thing as difficult to me
    To will the let of love where will my love hath set,
    As you to will to set love where will is your let?
Loved-not-loving.
    Well said, and put case it as hard now be
    For you to will to leave her, as for me
    To love him, yet have ye above me a mean
    To learn you at length to will to leave love clean,
    Which mean many thousands of lovers hath brought
    From right fervent loving to love right naught,
    Which long and oft-approved mean is absence;   980
    Whereto, when ye will, ye may have licence,
    Which I crave and wish and cannot obtain,
    For he will never my presence refrain.
Lover-not-loved.
    This is a med'cine like as ye would will me
    For thing to cure me the thing that would kill me;
    For presence of her, though I seld when may have,
    Is, fool, the med'cine that my life doth save.
    Her absence can I with as illwill will
    As I can will to leave to love her still;
    Thus is this will brought in incident'lly,   990

79

No aid in your purpose worth tail of a fly,
And as concerning our principal matter
All that ye lay may be laid even a' water.
I wonder that shame suffereth you to compare
With my pain, since ye are driven to declare
That all your pain is but sight and hearing
Of him, that as I do, dieth in pain feeling.
O pain upon pain! What pains I sustain!
No craft of the devil can express all my pain;
In this body no limb, joint, sinew, nor vein,   1000
But mart'reth each other, and this brain
Chief enmy of all, by the inventing
Mine unsavoury suit to her discontenting.
My speaking, my hearing, my looking, my thinking,
In sitting, in standing, in waking, or winking,
Whatever I do, or wherever I go,
My brain and mishap in all these do me woe.
As for my senses, each one of all five
Wond'reth, as it can, to feel itself alive;
And then hath love gotten all in one bed   1010
Himself and his servants, to lodge in this head:
Vain hope, despair, dread, and audacity,
Haste, waste, lust without liking or liberty,
Diligence, humility, trust, and jealousy,
Desire, patient sufferance, and constancy—
These with other, in this head like swarms of bees
Sting in debating their contrarieties;
The venom whereof from this head distilleth
Down to this breast, and this heart it killeth.
All times in all places of this body,   1020
By this distemperance thus distempered am I:
Shivering in cold, and yet in heat I die,
Drowned in moisture, parched parchment dry.
No-lover-nor-loved.
Cold, hot, moist, dry, in all places at once?
Marry sir, this is an ague for the nonce.
But or we give judgement, I must search to view
Whether this evidence be false or true.
Nay, stand still, your part shall prove never the warse;
So, by Saint Saviour here is a hot arse!
Let me feel your nose—nay fear not man, be bold: 1030

Well, though this arse be warm and this nose cold,
Yet these twain by attorney brought in one place
Are as he saieth, cold and hot both in like case.
Oh what pain drought is! See how his dry lips
Smack for more moisture of his warm moist hips.
Breathe out; these eyes are dull but this nose is quicker:
Here is most moisture, your breath smelleth of liquor.

Loved-not-loving.

Well since ye have opened in this tale telling
The full of your pain, for speed to ending
I shall in few words such one question disclose,   1040
As if your answer give cause to suppose
The whole of the same to be answered at full,
We need no judgement, for yield myself I wull.
Put case this man loved a woman, such one
Who were in his liking the thing alone,
And that his love to her were not so mickle
But her fancy toward him were as little,
And that she hid herself, so day and night
That seld time when he might come in her sight;
And then put case that one to you love did bear,   1050
A woman that other so ugly were
That each kiss of her mouth called you to Gib's feast,
Or that your fancy abhorred her so at least,
That her presence were as sweet to suppose
As one should present—

No-lover-nor-loved.   A turd to his nose?

Loved-not-loving.

Yea, in good faith; whereto the case is this,
That her spiteful presence absent never is.
Of these two cases if chance should drive you
To choose one, which would ye choose? Tell truth now.   1060
What, ye study?

No-lover-nor-loved. Tarry, ye be too greedy;
Men be not like women, alway ready.

Lover-not-loved.

In good sooth, to tell truth of these cases twain
Which case is the worst is to me uncertain.

Loved-not-loving.

First case of these twain I put for your part,
And by the last case appeareth mine own smart;

If they proceed with this first case of ours
Then is our matter undoubtedly yours,
And if judgement pass with this last case in fine,   1070
Then is the matter assuredly mine.
Since by these cases our parts so do seem
That which is most painful yourself cannot deem,
If ye now will all circumstance eschew,
Make this question in these cases our issue,
And the pain of these men to abbreviate,
Set all our other matter as frustrate.
Lover-not-loved. Agreed.
Loved-not-loving.
Then further to abridge your pain,
Since this our issue appeareth thus plain,   1080
As folk not doubting your conscience nor cunning,
We shall in the same let pass all reasoning,
Yielding to your judgement the whole of my part.
Lover-not-loved.
And I likewise mine, with will and good heart.
No-lover-nor-loved.
So, lo, make you low curtsy to me now,
And straight I will make as low curtsy to you.
Nay, stand ye near the upper end I pray ye,
For the nether end is good enough for me.
Your cases which include your grief each whit
Shall dwell in this head.   1090
Lover-loved.   •   And in mine, but yet
Or that we herein our judgement publish,
I shall desire you that we twain may finish
As far in our matter toward judgement
As ye have done in yours, to the intent
That we our parts brought together thither,
May come to judgement fro thence togither.
No-lover-nor-loved. By'r Lady sir, and I desire the same.
Loved-not-loving. I would ye began.
Lover-not-loved.   Begin then, in God's name.   1100
Lover-loved. Shall I begin?
No-lover-nor-loved.   Since I look but for winning,
Give me the end and take you the beginning.
Lover-loved.
Who shall win the end, the end at end shall try.

For my part whereof now thus begin I:
I am as I said, a beloved lover,
And he no lover nor beloved nother,
In which two cases he maketh his avaunt
Of both our parts to prove his most pleasant,
But be ye assured by aught I yet see,   1110
In his estate no manner pleasure can be.

No-lover-nor-loved.

Yes, two manner pleasures ye must needs confess:
First I have the pleasure of quietness,
And the second is I am contented.

Lover-loved.

That second pleasure now secondly invented;
To compare with pleasure by contentation
Is a very second imagination.

No-lover-nor-loved.

Then show your wit for proof of this in hand:
How may pleasure without contentation stand?

Lover-loved.

Pleasure without contentation cannot be,   1120
But contentation without pleasure we see
In things innumerable every day,
Of all which mark these which I shall now lay:
Put case that I for pleasure of some friend,
Or some thing which I longed to see at end,
Would be content to ride threescore mile this night
And never would bate nor never alight,
I might be right well content to do this,
And yet in this doing no pleasure there is;
Moreover ye, by patient sufferance   1130
May be contented with any mischance,
The loss of your child, friend, or anything
That in this world to you can be longing,
Wherein, ye contented never so well,
Yet is your contentation pleasure no dell.

No-lover-nor-loved.

These two examples, by aught that I see
Be nothing the things that anything touch me.
With death of my child my being contented,
Or pain with my friend willingly assented,
Is not contentation voluntary,   1140

For that contentation cometh forcibly;
But my contentation standeth in such thing
As I would first wish, if it went by wishing.
Lover-loved.
    Sir, be ye contented even as ye tell,
Yet your contentation can nother excell
Nor be compared equal to mine estate,
For touching contentation, I am in rate
As highly contented to love as ye see,
As ye to forbear love can wish to be.
Had I no more to say in this argument   1150
But that I am as well as you content,
Yet hath my part now good approbation
To match with yours even by contentation.
But contentation is not all the thing
That I for my love have in recompensing;
Above contentation, pleasures feeling
Have I so many, that no wight living
Can by any wit or tongue the same report.
Oh, the pleasant pleasures in our resort!
After my being from her any whither,   1160
What pleasures have we in coming togither!
Each tap on the ground toward me with her fote
Doth bathe in delight my very heart rote,
Every twink of her alluring eye
Reviveth my spirits even thoroughoutly,
Each word of her mouth not a preparative,
But the right medicine or preservative.
We be so jocund and joyfully joined,
Her love for my love so currently coined,
That all pleasures earthly, the truth to declare,   1170
Are pleasures not able with ours to compare.
This mouth in manner receiveth no food;
Love is the feeding that doth this body good,
And this head despiseth all these eyes winking
Longer than love doth keep this heart thinking
To dream on my sweetheart. Love is my feeder;
Love is my lord, and love is my leader.
Of all mine affairs in thought, word, and deed,
Love is the Christ's cross that must be my speed.

No-lover-nor-loved.

By this I perceive well ye make reckoning   1180
That love is a godly and a good thing.

Lover-loved.

Love good? What ill in love canst thou make appear?

No-lover-nor-loved.

Yes, I shall prove this love at this time meant here
In this man's case as ill as is the devil,
And in your case I shall prove love more evil.
What tormentry could all the devils in hell
Devise to his pain that he doth not tell?
What pain bringeth that body those devils in that head,
Which ministers alway by love are led?
He freezeth in fire, he drowneth in drought,   1190
Each part of his body love hath brought about;
Where each to help other should be diligent,
They martyr each other the man to torment.
Without stint of rage his pains be so sore
That no fiend may torment man in hell more.
And, as in your case, to prove that love is
Worse than the devil, my meaning is this;
Love distempereth him by torment in pain,
And love distempereth you as far in joy plain.
Your own confession declareth that ye   1200
Eat, drink, or sleep even as little as he,
And he that lacketh any one of those three,
Be it by joy or by pain, clear ye see
Death must be sequel however it be;
And thus are ye both brought by love's induction,
By pain or by joy to like point of destruction;
Which point approveth love in this case past
Beyond the devil in tormentry to have a cast;
For I trow ye find naught that the devil can find
To torment man in hell by any pleasant mind,   1210
Whereby as I said I say of love still:
Of the devil and love, love is the more ill.
And at beginning I may say to yow,
If God had seen as much as I say now
Love had been Lucifer, and doubt ye no whit
But experience now hath taught God such wit,
That if aught come at Lucifer other than good,

85

To whip souls on the breech love shall be the blood.
And sure he is one that cannot live long,
For aged folk ye wot well cannot be strong; 1220
And another thing his physician doth guess—
That he is infect with the black jaundice.

Lover-loved.

No further then, ye be infect with folly,
For in all these words no word can I espy
Such as for your part any proof avoucheth.

No-lover-nor-loved.

For proof of my part? No, but it toucheth
The disproof of yours, for where you alleged
Your part above mine to be compared,
By pleasures in which your displeasures are such
That ye eat, drink, nor sleep, or at most not much, 1230
In lack whereof my tale proveth plainly
Each part of your pleasure a tormentry,
Whereby your good love I have proved so evil
That love is apparently worse than the devil.
And as touching my part, there can arise
No manner displeasures nor tormentries
In that I love not, nor am not loved:
I move no displeasures nor none to me moved,
But all displeasures of love fro me absent,
By absence whereof I quietly content. 1240

Lover-loved.

Sir where ye said, and think ye have said well
That my joy by love shall bring death in sequel,
In that by the same in manner I disdain
Food and sleep, this proverb answereth you plain:
Look not on the meat, but look on the man.
Now look ye on me, and say what ye can.

No-lover-nor-loved.

Nay, for a time love may puff up a thing,
But lacking food and sleep death is the ending.

Lover-loved.

Well sir, till such time as death approve it,
This part of your tale may sleep every whit, 1250
And where ye by absent displeasure wold
Match with my present pleasure, ye seem more bold
Than wise, for those twain be far different sure.

No-lover-nor-loved. Is not absence of displeasure a pleasure?
Lover-loved.
    Yes, in like rate as a post is pleased—
    Which, as by no mean it can be diseased
    By displeasure present, so is it true
    That no pleasure present in it can ensue.
    Pleasures or displeasures feeling sensibly,
    A post ye know well, cannot feel possibly,   1260
    And as a post in this case I take you,
    Concerning the effect of pleasure in hand now;
    For any feeling ye in pleasure endure,
    More than ye say ye feel in displeasure.
No-lover-nor-loved.
    Sir though the effect of your pleasure present
    Be more pleasant than displeasure absent,
    Yet how compare ye with mine absent pain
    By present displeasures in which ye remain?
Lover-loved. My present displeasures? I know none such.
No-lover-nor-loved. Know ye no pain by love little nor much?   1270
Lover-loved. No.
No-lover-nor-loved.
    Then shall I show such a thing in this purse
    As shortly shall show herein your part the worse.
    Now I pray God the devil in hell blind me—
    By the mass I have left my book behind me.
    I beseech our Lord I never go hence
    If I would not rather have spent fortypence;
    But since it is thus, I must go fetch it.
    I will not tarry; ah sir, the devil stretch it!
Lover-loved. Farewell dawcock.   1280
No-lover-nor-loved.   Farewell woodcock.

           [*Exit No-lover-nor-loved.*]

Lover-loved.   He is gone.
Loved-not-loving. Gone, yea, but he will come again anon.
Lover-loved.
    Nay, this night he will no more disease you;
    Give judgement hardily even when it please you;
    Which done, sith he is gone, myself straight shall
    Righteously between you give judgement final.
    But lord, what a face this fool hath set here

Till shame defaced his folly so clear!
That shame hath shamefully in sight of you all   1290
With shame driven him hence to his shameful fall;
Wherein, although I naught gain by winning
That aught may augment my pleasure in loving,
Yet shall I win thereby a pleasure to see
That ye all shall see the matter pass with me.
What though the profit may lightly be loaden?
It grieveth a man to be overtrodden.
Nay, when I saw that his winning must grow
By pain pretending in my part to show,
Then wist I well the noddy must come   1300
To do as he did, or stand and play mum.
No man, no woman, no child in this place
But I durst for judgement trust in this case.
All doubt of my pain by his proof by any mean,
His running away hath now scraped out clean;
Wherefore give judgement and I shall return
In place here by where my dear heart doth sojourn;
And after salutation between us had
(Such as is meet to make lovers' hearts glad)
I shall, to rejoice her in merry tidings,   1310
Declare the whole rabble of this fool's leasings.

*Here the Vice cometh in running suddenly about the place among the
audience with a high coppintank on his head full of squibs fired crying
'Water water, fire fire, fire, water, water, fire,' till the fire in the squibs
be spent.*

Lover-loved. Water and fire?
No-lover-nor-loved.   Nay, water for fire I mean!
Lover-loved.
   Well, thanked be God it is out now clean.
   How came it there?
No-lover-nor-loved.   Sir, as I was going
   To fet my book for which was my departing,
   There chanced in my way a house here by
   To fire which is burned piteously;   1320
   But marvelously the people do moan
   For a woman—they say a goodly one—
   A sojourner, whom in this house burned is.
   And shouting of the people for help in this

Made me run thither to have done some good;
And at a window thereof as I stood,
I thrust in my head, and even at a flush
Fire flashed in my face and so took my bush.
Lover-loved. What house?
No-lover-nor-loved. A house painted with red ochre;   1330
The owner whereof they say is a broker.
Lover-loved.
Then, break heart! Alas, why live I this day?
My dear heart is destroyed, life and wealth away!
No-lover-nor-loved.
What man? Sit down and be of good cheer.
God's body, Master Woodcock is gone clear.
Oh Master Woodcock, fair mot befall ye;
Of right Master Woodcock I must now call ye.
Mistress, stand you here afore and rub him,
And I will stand here behind and dub him.
Nay, the child is asleep, ye need not rock.   1340
Master Woodcock! Master wood wood Woodcock!
Where folk be far within, a man must knock;
Is not this a pang, trow ye, beyond the nock?
Speak Master Woodcock, speak parrot I pray ye;
My leman your lady aye will ye see.
My lady your leman, one undertakes,
To be safe from fire by slipping through a jakes.
Lover-loved. That word I heard, but yet I see her not.
No-lover-nor-loved. No more do I, Master Woodcock, our Lord
Lover-loved.   wot.
Unto that house where I did see her last,   1350
I will seek to see her, and if she be passed,
So that to appear there I cannot make her,
Then will I burn after and overtake her.

The Lover loved goeth out.

No-lover-nor-loved.
Well, ye may burn together for all this,
And do well enough for aught that is yet amiss.
For God's sake, one run after and baste him;
It were great pity the fire should waste him,
For being fat, your knowledge must record,
A woodcock well roast is a dish for a lord.

89

And for a woodcock ye all must now know him 1360
By matter of record that so doth show him;
And briefly to bring you all out of doubt,
All this have I feigned to bring about
Himself to convince himself even by act,
As he hath done here in doing this fact.
He taketh more thought for this one woman now
Than could I for all in the world, I make a vow;
Which hath so shamefully defaced his part
That to return, nother hath he face nor heart.
Which seen, whiles he and she lose time in kissing, 1370
Give ye with me judgement a' God's blessing.

[*Lover-loved enters*]

Lover-loved.
The proof of my saying at my first entry
That wretch bringeth now in place, in that I laid
Dissembling man's mind by appearance to be
Thing inconvenient, which thing as I said
Is proved now true. How was I dismayed
By his false facing the death of my darling,
Whom, I thank God, is in health and aileth nothing!
No-lover-nor-loved.
Sir I beseech you, of all your dismaying
What other cause can ye lay than your loving? 1380
Lover-loved. My loving? Nay, all the cause was your lying.
No-lover-nor-loved. What had my lie done if ye had not loved?
Lover-loved. What did my love till your lie was moved?
No-lover-nor-loved.
By these two questions it seemeth we may make
Your love and my lie to part evenly the stake.
Loving and lying have we brought now hither,
Lovers and liars to lie both togither.
But put case my lie of her death were true,
What excuse for your love could then ensue?
Lover-loved.
If fortune (God save her) did bring her to it, 1390
The fault were in fortune and in love no whit.
No-lover-nor-loved.
The whole fault in fortune? By my sheath well hit;
God send your fortune better than your wit.

90

Lover-loved.

Well sir, at extremity I can prove
The fault in fortune as much as in love.

No-lover-nor-loved.

Then fortune in like case with love now join yow
As I with loving joined lying even now,
And well they may join all by aught that I see,
For each of all three I take like vanity.
But since ye confess that your part of such pain   1400
Cometh half by love, and that it is certain
That certain pains to loved lovers do move,
In which the fault in nothing save only love;
As dread and jealousy, each of which with mo,
To your estate of love is a daily foe,
And I clear out of love declaring such show,
As in my case no pain to me can grow,
I say this considered hath pith sufficient
In proof of my part to drive you to judgement.

Lover-loved.

Nay, first a few words. Sir, though I confess   1410
That love bringeth some pain, and your case painless
By mean of your contented quietness,
Yet th'actual pleasures that I possess
Are as far above the case that ye profess,
As is my pain, in your imagination,
Under the pleasures of contentation.
Thus, wade how ye will one way or other,
If ye win one way ye shall lose another;
But if ye intend for end to be brief,
Join with me herein for indifferent prefe: 1420
A tree ye know well is a thing that hath life,
And such a thing as never feeleth pain or strife,
But ever quiet and alway contented;
And as there can no way be invented
To bring a tree displeasure by feeling pain,
So no feeling pleasure in it can remain.
A horse is a thing that hath life also,
And he by feeling feeleth both wealth and woe;
By driving or drawing all day in the mire
Many painful journeys hath he in hire,   1430
But after all those he hath alway at night

These pleasures following, to his great delight:
First, fair washed at a river or a weir,
And straight brought to a stable warm and fair;
Dry rubbed and chafed from head to heel,
And curried till he be slick as an eel.
Then he is littered in manner nose high,
And hay, as much as will in his belly;
Then provender hath he, oats, peas, beans, or bread,
Which feeding in feeling as pleasant to his head,   1440
As to a covetous man to behold
Of his own Westminster Hall full of gold.
After which feeding he sleepeth in quiet rest
During such time as his meat may digest.
All this considered, a horse or a tree,
If ye must choose the ton, which would ye be?
No-lover-nor-loved.
When the horse must to labour, by our Lady
I had lever be a tree than a horse, I.
Lover-loved.
But how when he resteth and filleth his gorge?
No-lover-nor-loved.
Then would I be a horse and no tree, by Saint George.   1450
Lover-loved.
But what if ye must needs stick to the ton?
No-lover-nor-loved.
Which were then best? By the mass I can name none.
Lover-loved.
The first case is yours and the next is for me.
In case like a tree I may liken ye,
For as a tree hath life without feeling,
Whereby it feeleth pleasing nor displeasing,
And cannot be but contented quietly,
Even the like case is yours now presently.
And as the horse feeleth pain and not the tree,
Likewise I have pain and no pain have ye;   1460
And as a horse above a tree feeleth pleasure,
So feel I pleasure above you in rate sure;
And as the tree feeleth nother and the horse both,
Even so pleasure and pain between us twain goeth.
Since these two cases so indifferently fall
That yourself can judge nother for partial,

For indifferent end I think this way best;
Of all our reasoning to debar the rest,
And in these two cases this one question
To be the issue that we shall join on.   1470
No-lover-nor-loved. Be it so.
Lover-loved.   Now are these issues couched so nie
That both sides I trust shall take end shortly.
Lover-not-loved.
    I hope and desire the same, and since we
    Were first heard, we both humbly beseech ye
    That we in like wise may have judgement first.
Lover-loved. I grant.
No-lover-nor-loved.   By the mass, and I, come best or worst.
Lover-loved.
    Though nature force man stiffly to incline
    To his own part in each particular thing,   1480
    Yet reason would man, when man shall determine
    Other men's parts by indifferent awarding,
    Indifferent to be in all his reasoning,
    Wherefore in this part cut we off affection,
    So that indifferency be direction.
No-lover-nor-loved.
    Contented with that, and by aught I espy
    We may in this matter take end quickly.
    Scan we their cases as she did apply them
    That we may perceive what is meant by them:
    He loveth unloved a goodly one,   1490
    She is loved not loving of an ugly one,
    Or in his eye his lover seemeth goodly,
    And in her eye her lubber seemeth as ugly.
    Her most desired angel's face he can not see;
    His most loathely hell-hound's face she cannot flee.
    He loveth, she abhorreth, whereby presence is
    His life, her death, whereby I say even this:
    Be his feeling pains in every degree
    As great and as many as he saith they be,
    Yet in my judgement by these cases hath she   1500
    As great and as many feeling pains as he.
Lover-loved.
    When matter at full is indifferently laid
    As ye in this judgement have laid this now,

93

What reason the time by me should be delayed?
Ye have spoken my thought, wherefore to you
In piecing your pains my conscience doth allow
A just counterpoise, and thus your pains be
Adjudged by us twain one pain in degree.
Lover-not-loved.
Well since your conscience driveth you thus to judge,
I receive this judgement without grief or grudge.   1510
Loved-not-loving.
And I in like rate, yielding unto you twain
Hearty thanks for this your undeserved pain.
Lover-not-loved.
Now, mistress, may it please you to declare
As touching their parts of what mind ye are?
Loved-not-loving.
With right good will sir, and sure I suppose
Their parts in few words may come to point well.
The two examples which he did disclose
All errors or doubts do clearly expel.
The estate of a tree his estate doth tell,
And of the horse his tale well understand   1520
Declareth as well his case now in hand;

For as nothing can please or displease a tree
By any pleasure or displeasure feeling,
Nor never bring a tree discontent to be,
So like case to him, not loved nor loving.
Love can no way bring pleasing or displeasing:
Live women, die women, sink women, or swim,
In all he content, for all is one to him.

And as a horse hath many painful journeys,
A lover best loved hath pains in like wise,   1530
As here hath appeared by sundry ways,
Which showeth his case in worst part to rise:
But then as the horse feeleth pleasure in size
At night in the stable, above the tree,
So feeleth he some pleasure as far above ye.

In some case he feeleth much more pleasure than he,
And in some case he feeleth even as much less;
Between the more and the less it seemeth to me

That between their pleasures no choice is to guess,
Wherefore I give judgement in short process: 1540
Set the ton pleasure even to the tother.
No-lover-nor-loved.
Womanly spoken, mistress, by the rood's mother.

Lover-not-loved.
Who heareth this tale with indifferent mind,
And seeth of these twain each one so full bent
To his own part, that nother in heart can find
To change pleasures with other, must needs assent
That she in these words hath given right judgement,
In affirmance whereof I judge and award
Both these pleasures of yours as one in regard.

Lover-loved.
Well since I think ye both without corruption,   1550
I shall move no matter of interruption.
No-lover-nor-loved.
Nor I, but masters, though I say naught in this,
May I not think my pleasure more than his?
Loved-not-loving.
Affection unbridled may make us all think
That each of us hath done other wrong,
But where reason taketh place it cannot sink,
Since cause to be partial here is none us among.
That one head that would think his own wit so strong,
That on his judges he might judgement devise,
What judge in so judging could judge him wise?   1560
Lover-loved.
Well, mine estate right well contenteth me.
No-lover-nor-loved.
And I with mine as well content as ye.

Lover-not-loved.
So should ye both likewise be contented
Each other to see content, in such degree
As on your parts our judgement hath awarded;
Your neighbour in pleasure like yourself to be,
Gladly to wish Christ's precept doth bind ye.
Thus contentation should alway prefer
One man to joy the pleasure of another.

Lover-loved.
    True, and contentation may be in like case,   1570
Although no health, yet help and great relief
In both your pains, for ye having such grace
To be contented in sufferance of grief,
Shall by contentation avoid much mischief
Such as the contrary shall surely bring you:
Pain to pain as painful as your pain is now.

Thus not we four but all the world beside,
Knowing themself or other in joy or pain,
Have need of contentation for a guide.
Having joy or pain, content let us remain;   1580
In joy or pain of other flee we disdain.
Be we content wealth or woe, and each for other
Rejoice in the ton and pity the tother.

Lover-not-loved.
    Since such contentation may hardly accord
In such kind of love as here hath been meant,
Let us seek the love of that loving Lord
Who to suffer passion for love was content,
Whereby his lovers, that love for love assent,
Shall have in fine above contentation
The feeling pleasure of eternal salvation.   1590

Which Lord of lords, whose joyful and blessed birth
Is now remembered by time presenting
This accustomed time of honest mirth,
That Lord we beseech in most humble meaning,
That it may please him by merciful hearing
Th'estate of this audience long to endure
In mirth, health, and wealth, to grant his pleasure.

AMEN

Printed by W. Rastell
M.ccccc.xxxiiii.
Cum privilegio Regali.

An Enterlude called Lusty Iuuentus.

Liuely describyng the frailtie of youth:
of nature, prone to vyce: by grace
and good councell trayn-
able to vertue.

The Personages that speake,
Messenger.
Lusty Iuuentus
Good councell.
Knowledge.
Sathan the Deuyl.
Hypocrisie.
Felowshyp.
Abhominable liuing.
Gods mercyfull promyses

Foure may play it easely, takyng such par
tes as they thinke best: so that any one tak
of those partes that be not in place at once.

AN INTERLUDE CALLED
LUSTY JUVENTUS

The Prologue of the Messenger.

Forasmuch as man is naturally prone	*Gen. 8*
To evil from his youth, as Scripture doth recite,	*Jere. 17*

Forasmuch as man is naturally prone   *Gen. 8*
To evil from his youth, as Scripture doth recite,   *Jere. 17*
It is necessary that he be speedily withdrawn
From concupiscence of sin, his natural appetite.
An order to bring up youth, Ecclesiasticus doth write: *Ecclus. 30*
An untamed horse will be hard saith he,
And a wanton child wilful will be.
Give him no liberty in youth, nor his folly excuse;
Bow down his neck and keep him in good awe
Lest he be stubborn; no labour refuse   10
To train him to wisdom and teach him God's law;
For youth is frail and easy to draw
By grace to goodness, by nature to ill:
That nature hath engrafted is hard to kill.
Nevertheless, in youth men may be best
Trained to virtue by Godly mean;
Vice may be so mortified and so suppressed
That it shall not break forth, yet the root will remain,
As in this Enterlude by Youth you shall see plain;
From his lust by Good Counsel brought to godly
   conversation,   20
And shortly after to frail nature's inclination.
The enemy of mankind, Satan, through Hypocrisy,
Feigned or chosen holiness of man's blind intent,
Forsaking God's word that leadeth the right way
Is brought to Fellowship and ungracious company:
To Abominable Living till he be wholly bent,
And so to desperation, if Good Counsel were not sent
From God, that in trouble doth no man forsake
That doth call and trust in him for Christ's sake.
Finally, Youth by God's special grace,   30
Doth earnestly repent his abominable living
By the doctrine of Good Counsel, and to his solace
God's Mercy entreth to him reciting

God's merciful promises as they be in writing.
He believeth and followeth to his great consolation.
All these parts ye shall see briefly played in their fashion.

[Exit Prologue.] Here entreth Lusty Juventus, or Youth singing as followeth.

In a Herber green asleep where as I lay,
The birds sang sweet in the mids of the day,
I dreamed fast of mirth and play,
In youth is pleasure, in youth is pleasure.   40
    Methought I walked still to and fro,
And fiom her company I could not go,
But I when I waked it was not so,
In youth is pleasure, in youth is pleasure.
    Therefore my heart is surely pight
Of her alone to have a sight,
Which is my joy and heart's delight,
In youth is pleasure, in youth is pleasure.   FINIS

Lusty Juventus or Youth he speaketh.

What ho! are they not here?
I am disappointed by the blessed mass;   50
I had thought to have found them making good cheer,
But now they are gone to some secret place.
Well, seeing they are gone I do not greatly pass,
Another time I will hold them as much,
Seeing they break promise and keep not the touch.
What shall I do now to pass away the day?
Is there any man here that will go to game?
At whatsoever he will play
To make one I am ready to the same.
Youth full of pleasure is my proper name;   *Naming*   60
To be alone is not my appety,
For of all things in the world I love merry company.
Who knoweth where is e'er a minstrel?
By the mass I would fain go dance a fit;
My companions are at it I know right well:
They do not all this while in a corner sit.
Against another time they have taught me wit.
I beshrew their hearts for serving me this;
I will go seek them whether I hit or miss.

99

Well I met father, well I met;   70
Did you hear any minstrels play
As you came hitherward upon your way?
And if you did I pray you wish me thither,
For I am going to seek them, and in faith I know not whither.
Good Coun. Sir I will ask you a question by your favour:
    What would you with the minstrel do?
Juven. Nothing but have a dance or two,
    To pass the time away in pleasure.
Good Coun. If that be the matter, I promise you sure
    I am the more sorrier that it should so be,   80
    For there is no such passing the time appointed in the
    Nor yet thereunto it doth not agree.   Scripture,
    I wish that ye would so use your liberty
    To walk as you are bound to do,
    According to the vocation which God hath called you to.
Juven. Why sir, are you angry because I have spoken so?
    By the mass it is alone for my appety.
Good Coun. Show me your name I pray you heartily,
    And then I will my mind express.
Juven. My name is called Juventus, doubtless;   90
    Say what you will, I will give you the hearing.
Good Coun. Forasmuch as God hath created you of nothing,
    Unto his own likeness by spiritual illumination,
    It is unmeet that ye should lead your living
    Contrary to his godly determination.
    Saint Paul unto the Ephesians giveth good exhortation
    Saying, walk circumspectly, redeeming the time:
    That is, to spend it well and not to wickedness incline.
Juven. No no, hardly none of mine;
    If I would live so straight you might count me a fool.   100
    Let them keep those rules which are Doctors divine,
    And have been brought up all their days in school.
Good Coun. Moses in the law exhorteth his people,
    As in the book of Deuteronomy he doth plainly write,
    That they should live obedient and thankful;
    For in effect these words he doth recite:
    All ye this day stand before the Lord's sight,
    Both princes, rulers, elders and parents,

Children, wives, young, and old: therefore obey his
    commandments.
Juven. I <u>am too</u> young to understand his documents;   110
    Wherefore di<u>d all they stand before his presence</u>?
Good Coun. To enter with God peace and alliance,
    Promising that they would him honour, fear, and serve.
    All kind of people were bound in those covenants
    That from his law they should never swerve,
    For God useth no partiality.
Juven. What, am I bound as well as the clergy,
    To learn and follow his precepts and law?
Good Coun. Yea, surely, or else God will withdraw
    His mercy from you promised in his covenant;   120
    For except you live under his obedience and awe,
    How can you receive the benefits of his Testament?
    For he that submitteth himself to be a servant,
    And his master's commandment will not fulfil nor regard,
    According as he hath done, is worthy his reward.
Juven. It is as true a saying as ever I heard,
    Therefore your name I pray you now tell,
    For by my truth your communication I like wonders well.
Good Coun. My name is called Good Counsel.
Juven. Good Counsel?   120
    Now in faith I cry you mercy;
    I am sorry that I have you thus offended,
    But I pray you bear with me patiently
    And my misbehaviour shall be amended.
    I know my time I have rudely spended
    Following my own lust, being led by ignorance,
    But now I hope of better knowledge through your
        acquaintance.
Good Coun. I pray God guide you with his gracious assistance,
    Unto the knowledge of his truth, your ignorance to undo,
    That you may be one of those numbered Christians,   140
    Which followeth the Lamb whither he doth go
    (The Lamb Jesus Christ, my meaning is so)
    By sure faith and confidence in his bitter death and passion,
    The only price of our health and salvation.
Juven. Sir, I thank you for your hearty oration,
    And now I pray you show me your advisement,
    How I may live in this my vocation

According to God's will and commandment.

Good Coun. First of all, it is most expedient
   That you exercise yourself in continual prayer, 150
   That it might please the Lord omnipotent
   To send unto you his Holy Spirit and Comforter,
   Which will lead you every day and hour
   Unto the knowledge of his word and verity,
   Wherein you may learn to live most christianly.

Juven. (*He kneeleth*) Oh Lord, grant me of thy infinite mercy
   The true knowledge of thy law and will,
   And illumine my heart with spirit continually,
   That I may be apt thy holy precepts to fulfil.
   Strengthen me, that I may persevere still 160
   Thy commandments to obey,
   And then I shall never slip nor fall away.   *He riseth.*

Good Coun. Full true be these words, which Christ himself did
   He that seeketh shall surely find.   say,   say,
   Behold Youth, now rejoice we may,
   For I see Knowledge of God, Verity, stand here behind.

Knowledge entreth.

He is come now to satisfy your mind
In those things which you will desire;
Therefore together let us approach him near.

Juven. Ah, Good Counsel, now it doth appear 170
   That God never rejecteth the humblest petition.

Know. Now the Lord bless you all with his heavenly benediction,
   And with his fiery love your hearts inflame,
   That of his merciful promises you may have the fruition,
   The subtlety of the Devil utterly to defame.
   Now, good Christian audience, I will express my name:
   The true Knowledge of God's verity, this my name doth hight,
   Whom God hath appointed to give the blind their sight.

Good Coun. All praise be given to that Lord of might,
   Which hath appointed you hither at this present hour, 180
   For I trust you will so instruct Youth aright,
   That he shall live according to God's pleasure.

Juven. And I thank Jesus Christ my saviour
   That he is come to my company.

Know. I thank you my friends most heartily,
   For your gentle salutation.

Juven. Sir I will be so bold by your deliberation
   To open my mind unto you now,
   Trusting that by your good exhortation
   I shall learn those things which I never knew.   190
   This one thing chiefly I would learn of you,
   How I may my life in this my vocation lead
   According as God hath ordained and decreed.
Know. The prophet David saith that the man is blessed
   Which doth exercise himself in the law of the Lord,
   And doth not follow the way of the wicked,
   As the first psalm doth plainly record.
   The four score and fourteenth psalm thereunto doth accord:
   Blessed is the man whom thou teachest oh Lord, saith he,
   To learn thy law, precepts, word, or verity;   200
   And Christ in the Gospel saith manifestly,
   Blessed is he which heareth the word of God and keepeth it;
   That is, to believe his word and live accordingly,
   Declaring the faith by the fruits of the spirit;
   Whose fruits are these, as Saint Paul to the Galathi doth
   Love, joy, peace, long suffering, and faithfulness,   write:
   Meekness, goodness, temperance, and gentleness.
Good Coun. By these words, which unto you he doth express,
   He teacheth that you ought to have a steadfast faith,
   Without the which it is impossible doubtless   210
   To please God, as Saint Paul saith.
   Where faith is not, godly living decayeth,
   For whatsoever is not of faith, saith Saint Paul, is sin,
   But where a perfect faith is, there is good working.
Juven. It seemeth to me that this is your meaning:
   That when I observe God's commandments and the works
   They shall prevail unto me nothing   of charity,
   Except I believe to be saved thereby.
Know. No no, you are deceived very blindly,
   For faith in Christ's merits doth only justify   220
   And make us righteous in God's sight.   < Protestant
                                                       emphasis
Juven. Why should I then in good works delight,
   Seeing I shall not be saved by them?
Good Coun. Because they are required of all Christian men
   As the necessary fruits of true repentance.
Know. But the reward of the heavenly inheritance
   Is given us through faith, for Christ's deservings,

103

As Saint Paul declareth in the fourth chapter to the Romans;
Therefore we ought not to work as hirelings.
Seeing Christ hath purged us once from all our wicked living   230
Let us no more wallow therein,
But persever like good branches bearing fruit in him.
Juven. Now I know whereabout you have been;
My elders never taught me so before.
Good Coun. Though your elders were blind, doubt not you
therefore;
For Saint Peter saith, vain is the conversations
Which ye receive by your elders' traditions.
Juven. I will gladly receive your godly admonitions,
But yet I pray you show me the cause
That they, being men of great discretions,   240
Did not instruct me in God's laws,
According to his will and ordinance.
Know. Because they themselves were wrapped in ignorance,
Being deceived by false preachers.
Juven. Oh Lord, deliver me from wicked teachers,
That I be not deceived with their false doctrine.
Good Coun. To God's word you must only incline;
All other doctrine clean set apart.
Juven. Surely that I will, from the bottom of my heart;
And I thank the living God which hath given me the
knowledge   250
To know his doctrine from the false and pervert,
I being yet young and full tender of age;
And that he hath made me partaker of the heavenly
Of his own mercy, and not of my deserving;   inheritage
For Hell I have deserved by my sinful working.
I know right well my elders and parents
Have of a long time deceived be,
With blind hypocrisy and superstitious intents,
Trusting in their own works which is nothing but vanity.
Their steps shall not be followed for me.   260
Therefore I pray you show me a brief conclusion,
How I ought to live in Christian religion.
Know. The first beginning of wisdom, as saith the wise Solomon,
Is to fear God with all thy heart and power;
And then thou must believe all his promises without any
exception,

And that he will perform them both constant and sure;
And then, because he is thy only saviour
Thou must love him with all thy soul and mind,
   And thy neighbour as thyself, because he hath so assigned.
Juven. To love my neighbour as myself? I cannot be so kind.   270
   I pray you tell me what mean you?
Know. My meaning is as Christ saith, in the seventh chapter
   To do to him as you would be done to.   of Matthew,
Juven. I pray God give me grace so for to do,
   That unto his will I may be obedient.
Good Coun. Here you shall receive Christ's Testament,
   To comfort your conscience when need shall require.
   To learn the contents thereof, see that you be diligent,
   The which all Christian men ought to desire,
   For it is the well, or fountain most clear,   280
   Out of the which doth spring sweet consolation
   To all those which thirst after eternal salvation.
Know. Therein shall you find most wholesome preservation,
   Both in troubles, persecutions, sickness, and adversity,
   And a sure defence in the time of temptation,
   Against whom the Devil cannot prevail with all his army;
   And if you persever therein unfeignedly,
   It will set your heart at such quietness and rest,
   Which can never be turned with storms nor tempest.
Good Coun. With this thing you must neither flatter nor jest,   290
   But steadfastly believe it every day and hour,
   And let your conversation openly protest
   That of your heart it is the most precious treasure;
   And then your godly example shall other men procure
   To learn and exercise the same also.
   I pray God strengthen you so for to do.
Juven. Now for this godly knowledge which you have brought
   I beseech the living God to reward you again.   me to,
   From your company I will never depart nor go,
   So long as in this life I do remain;   300
   For in this book I see manifest and plain,
   That he that followeth his own lusts and imagination,
   Keepeth the ready path to everlast damnation,
   And he that leadeth a godly conversation,
   Shall be brought to such quietness, joy, and peace,
   Which in comparison passeth all worldly gloriation,

Which cannot endure but shortly cease.
Both the time and hour I may now bless,
That I met with you, father Good Counsel,
To bring me to the knowledge of this heavenly Gospel. 310

Know. This your profession I like very well,
So that you intend to live according.
I pray God your living do not rebel,
But ever agree unto your saying,
That when ye shall make accounts or reckoning
Of this talent which you have received,
You may be one of those with whom the Lord shall be
pleased.

Good Coun. For this conversation of Youth the Lord's name be
praised.
Let us now depart for a season. *Exit.*

Know. To give God the glory it is convenient and reason. 320
If you will depart I will not tarry. *Exit.*

Juven. And I will never forsake your company
While I live in this world. *Exit.*

Here entreth the Devil.

[*Devil*] Oh, oh, all too late!
I trow this gear will come to naught,
For I perceive my power doth abate,
For all the policy that ever I have wrought,
Many and sundry ways I have sought
To have the word of God deluded utterly.
Oh for sorrow, yet it will not be. 330
I have done the best that I can,
And my ministers also in every place,
To root it clean from the heart of man;
And yet for all that it flourisheth apace.
I am sore in dread to show my face,
My authority and works are so greatly despised,
My inventions, and all that ever I have devised.
Oh, oh, full well I know the cause
That my estimation doth thus decay;
The old people would believe still in my laws, 340
But the younger sort lead them a contrary way.
They will not believe, they plainly say,
In old traditions and made by men,

106

But they will live as the Scripture teacheth them.
Out I cry upon them, they do me open wrong
To bring up their children thus in knowledge,
For if they will not follow my ways when they are young
It is hard turning them when they come to age.
I must needs find some means this matter to swage;
I mean to turn their hearts from the Scripture quite,   350
That in carnal pleasures they may have more delight.
Well I will go taste to infect this youth
Through the enticement of my son Hypocrisy,
And work some proper feat to stop his mouth
That he may lead his life carnally.
I had never more need my matters to apply.
Oh my child Hypocrisy, where art thou?
I charge thee of my blessing appear before me now.

Here entreth Hypocrisy.

Hypoc. Oh, oh, quod ha, keep again the sow!
  I come as fast as I can I warrant you.   360
  Where is he that hath the sow to sell?
  I will give him money if I like her well.
  Whether it be sow or hog I do not greatly care,
  For by my occupation I am a butcher.
Devil. Oh my child how dost thou fare?
Hypoc. Sancti amen! who have we there?
  By the mass I will buy none of thy ware;
  Thou art a chapman for the Devil.
Devil. What my son, canst thou not tell
  Who is here and what I am?   370
  I am thine own father Satan.
Hypoc. Be you so sir? I cry you mercy than.
  You may say I am homely and lack learning
  To liken my father's voice unto a sow's groaning;
  But I pray you show me the cause and why
  That you called me hither so hastily.
Devil. Ah Hypocrisy, I am undone utterly.
Hypoc. Utterly undone? Nay, stop there hardily,
  For I myself do know the contrary
  By daily experience.   380
  Do not I yet reign abroad?
  And as long as I am in the world

107

You have some treasure and substance.
I suppose I have been the flower
In setting forth thy laws and power
Without any delay.
By the mass, if I had not been,
Thou hadst not been worth a Flanders pin
At this present day.
The time were too long now to declare 390
How many and great the number are
Which have deceived be,
And brought clean from God's law,
Unto thy yoke and awe,
Through the enticement of me.
I have been busied since the world began
To graff thy laws in the heart of man,
Where they ought to be refused;
And I have so mingled God's commandments
With vain zeals and blind intents, 400
That they be greatly abused.
I set up great idolatry
With all kind of filth[y sodomitry],
To give [mankind a fall];
And I bro[ught up such superstition],
Under th[e name of holiness and religion],
That dec[eived almost all].
As holy [cardinals, holy popes],
Holy vesti[ments, holy copes],
Holy hermits and friars, 410
Holy priests, holy bishops,
Holy monks, holy abbots—
Yea, and all obstinate liars.
Holy pardons, holy beads,
Holy saints, holy images,
With holy holy blood,
Holy stocks, holy stones,
Holy clouts, holy bones,
Yea, and holy holy wood.
Holy skins, holy bulls, 420
Holy rochets and coals,
Holy crutches and staves,
Holy hoods, holy caps,

Holy mitres, holy hats,
Ah, good holy holy knaves!
Holy days, holy fastings,
Holy twitching, holy tastings,
Holy visions and sights,
Holy wax, holy lead,
Holy water, holy bread,   430
To drive away sprites.
Holy fire, holy palm,
Holy oil, holy cream,
And holy ashes also;
Holy brooches, holy rings,
[Holy kneeling], holy censings,
[And a hundred trim trams mo].
[Holy crosses, holy bells],
[Holy relics, holy jewels],
[Of mine own invention];   440
[Holy candles, holy tapers],
[Holy parchments, holy papers]:
[Had not you a holy son?]
Devil. All these things which thou hast done
My honour and laws hath maintained;
But now, oh alas, one thing is begun
By the which my kingdom is greatly decayed:
I shall lose all, I am sore afraid.
Except thy help I know right plain
I shall never be able to recover it again.   450
God's word is so greatly sprung up in youth
That he little regardeth my laws or me.
He telleth his parents, that is very truth,
That they of long time have deceived be;
He saith, according to Christ's verity
All his doings he will order and frame,
Mortifying the flesh with the lusts of the same.
Hypoc. Ah, sirrah, there beginneth the game!
What, is Juventus become so tame
To be a new gospeller?   460
Devil. As fast as I do make he doth mar.
He hath followed so long the steps of Good Counsel
That Knowledge and he together doth dwell;
For who is so busy in every place as Youth,

To read and declare the manifest truth?
But oh, Hypocrisy, if thou could stop his mouth
Thou shouldest win my heart for ever!

Hypoc. What would you have me to do in the matter?
Show me therein your advisement.

Devil. I would have thee go incontinent,   470
And work some craft, feat, or policy,
To set knowledge and him at controversy,
And his company thyself greatly use,
That God's word he may clean abuse.

Hypoc. At your request I will not refuse
To do that thing which in me doth lie;
Doubt ye not but I will excuse
Those things which he doth plainly deny,
And I will handle my matters so craftily,
That ere he cometh to man's state   480
God's word and his living shall be clean at the bate.

Devil. Thou shalt have my blessing both early and late;
And because thou shalt all my counsel keep
Thou shalt call thy name Friendship.

Hypoc. By the mass, it is a name full meet
For my proper and amiable person.

Devil. Oh farewell, farewell my son;
Speed thy business, for I must be gone.   *Exit.*

Hypoc. I warrant you, let me alone;
I will be with Juventus anon,   490
And that ere he be ware;
And iwis, if he walk not straight
I will use such a sleight
That shall trap him in a snare.
How shall I bring this gear to pass?
I can tell now, by the mass,
Without any more advisement:
I will infect him with wicked company,
Whose conversation shall be so fleshly,
Yea, able to overcome an innocent.   500
This wicked Fellowship
Shall him company keep
For awhile,
And then I will bring in
Abominable Living,

Him to beguile.
With words fair I will him 'tice,
Telling him of a girl nice,
Which shall him somewhat move,
Abominable Living though she be;   510
Yet he shall no other ways see
But she is for to love.
She shall him procure
To live in pleasure
After his own fantasy;
And my matter to frame
I will call her name
Unknown Honesty.
Thus will I convey
My matter, I say,   520
Somewhat handsomely,
That through wicked Fellowship
And false pretend Friendship,
Youth shall live carnally.
Trudge, Hypocrisy, trudge,
Thou art a good drudge
To serve the Devil:
If thou shouldest lie and lurk,
And not intend thy work,
Thy master should do full evil.   530

Here entreth Youth to whom Hypocrisy yet speaketh.

What, master Youth?
Well I met by my truth.
And whither away?
You are the last man
Which I talked on,
I swear by this day.
Methought by your face,
Ere you came in place,
It should be you;
Therefore I did abide   540
Here in this tide,
For your coming, this is true.
Juven. For your gentleness, sir, most heartily I thank you,
  But yet you must hold me somewhat excused,

For to my simple knowledge I never knew
That you and I together were acquainted;
But, nevertheless, if you do it renew,
Old acquaintance will soon be remembered.

Hypoc. Ah, now I see well Youth is feathered,
  And his crumbs he hath well gathered   550
  Since I spake with him last.
  A poor man's tale cannot now be heard
  As in times past.
  I cry you mercy, I was somewhat bold,
  Thinking that your mastership would
  Not have been so strange,
  But now I perceive that promotion
  Causeth both man, manners, and fashion,
  Greatly for to change.

Juven. You are to blame thus me to challenge,   560
  For I think I am not he which you take me for.

Hypoc. Yes, I have known you ever since you were bore:
  Your age is yet under a score,
  Which I can well remember.
  Iwis, iwis you and I
  Many a time have been full merry,
  When you were young and tender.

Juven. Then I pray you, let us reason no lenger,
  But first show your nomination.

Hypoc. Of my name to make declaration   570
  Without any dissimulation,
  I am called Friendship.
  Although I be simple and rude of fashion,
  Yet by lineage and generation
  I am nigh kin to your mastership.

Juven. What, Friendship?
  I am glad to see that you be merry;
  By my truth, I had almost you forgot
  By long absence brought out of memory.

Hypoc. By the mass, I love you so heartily   580
  That there is none so welcome to my company;
  I pray you tell me whither are you going?

Juven. My intention is to go hear a preaching.

Hypoc. A preaching quod ha? Ah, good little one,
  By Christ she will make you cry out of the winning,

If you follow her instructions so early in the morning.

Juven. Full great I do abhor this your wicked saying,
For no doubt they increase much sin and vice;
Therefore I pray you show not your meaning,
For I delight not in such foolish fantasies.   590

Hypoc. Surely then, you are the more unwise;
You may have a spurt amongst them now and then.
Why should not you as well as other men?

Juven. As for those filthy doings, I utterly detest them;
I will hear no more of your wicked communication.

Hypoc. If I may be so bold, by your deliberation,
What will you do at a preaching?

Juven. Learn some wholesome and godly teaching
Of the true minister of Christ's gospel.

Hypoc. Tush, what he will say I know right well;   600
He will say that God is a good man:
He can make him no better, and say the best he can.

Juven. I know that, but what then?
The more that God's word is preached and taught,
The greater the occasion is to all Christian men
To forsake their sinful livings both wicked, vile, and naught,
And to repent their former evils which they have wrought,
Trusting by Christ's death to be redeemed;
And he that this doth shall never be deceived.

Hypoc. Well said, Master Doctor, well said;   610
By the mass, we must have you into the pulpit.
I pray you be remembered and cover your head,
For indeed you have need to keep in your wit.
Ah, sirrah, who would have thought it
That Youth had been such a well-learned man?
Let me see your portas, gentle Sir John.

Juven. No, it is not a book for you to look on;
You ought not to jest with God's Testament.

Hypoc. What man, I pray you be content,
For I do nothing else but say my fantasy;   620
But yet if you would do after my advisement,
In that matter you should not be so busy.
Was not your father as well learned as ye?
And if he had said then as you have now done,
Iwis he had been like to make a burn.

Juven. It were much better for me then, to return

113

From my faith in Christ and the profession of his word?

Hypoc. Whether is better, a halter or a cord,
    I cannot tell, I swear by God's Mother,
    But I think you will have the one or the other.   630
    Will you lose all your friends' goodwill
    To continue in that opinion still?
    Was there not as well-learned men before as now?
    Yea, and better too, I may say to you;
    And they taught the younger sort of people
    By the elders to take an example.
    And if I did not love you as nature doth me bind,
    You should not know so much of my mind.

Juven. Whether were I better to be ignorant and blind,
    And to be damned in Hell for infidelity,   640
    Or to learn godly knowledge, wherein I shall find
    The right pathway to eternal felicity?

Hypoc. Can you deny but it is your duty
    Unto your elders to be obedient?

Juven. I grant I am bound to obey my parents
    In all things honest and lawful.

Hypoc. Lawful quod ha? Ah fool, fool,
    Wilt thou set men to school
    When they be old?
    I may say to you secretly,   650
    The world was never merry
    Since children were so bold;
    Now every boy will be a teacher,
    The father a fool, and the child a preacher:
    This is pretty gear!
    The foul presumption of Youth
    Will turn shortly to great ruth,
    I fear, I fear, I fear.

Juven. The sermon will be done ere I can come there;
    I care not greatly whether I go or no,   660
    And yet for my promise, by God I swear
    There is no remedy but I must needs go.
    Of my companions there will be mo,
    And I promised them by God's grace
    To meet them there as the sermon was.

Hypoc. For once breaking promise do not you pass;
    Make some excuse the matter to cease.

What have they to do?
And you and I were I wot where,
We would be as merry as there;   670
Yea, and merrier too.
Juven. I would gladly in your company go,
But if my companions should chance to see
They would report full evil by me;
And peradventure if I should it use,
My company they would clean refuse.
Hypoc. What, are those fellows so curious
That yourself you cannot excuse?
I will teach you the matter to convey:
Do what your own lust, and say as they say,   680
And if you be reproved with your own affinity,
Bid them pluck the beam out of their own eye.
The old popish priests mock and despise,
And the ignorant people that believe their lies,
Call them papists, hypocrites, and joining of the plough;
Face out the matter and then good enough.
Let your book at your girdle be tied,
Or else in your bosom that he may be spied,
And then it will be said both with youth and age,
Yonder fellow hath an excellent knowledge.   690
Tush, tush,
I could so beat the bush,
That all should be flush
That ever I did.
Juven. Now by my truth, you are merrily disposed.
Let us go thither as you think best.
Hypoc. How say you, shall we go to breakfast?
Will you go to the pie feast?
Or by the mass, if thou wilt be my guest
It shall cost thee nothing.   700
I have a furney card in a place
That will bear a turn besides the ace:
She purveys now apace
For my coming;
And if thou wilt jeopard as well as I
We shall have merry company,
And I warrant thee if we have not a pie,
We shall have a pudding.

Juven. By the mass that meat I love above all thing;
    You may draw me about the town with a pudding.   710
Hypoc. Then you shall see my cunning;
    A poor shift for a living
    Amongst poor men used is.
    The kind heart of hers
    Hath eased my purse,
    Many a time ere this.

Here entreth Fellowship.

[*Fellowship.*] I marvel greatly where Friendship is.
    He promised to meet me here ere this time;
    I beshrew his heart that his promise doth miss,
    And then be ye sure it shall not be mine.   720
Hypoc. Yes, Fellowship, that it shall be thine,
    For I have tarried here this hour or twain,
    And this honest gentleman in my company hath been
    To abide your coming, this thing is plain.
Fellow. By the mass, if you chide I wilt be gone again,
    For in faith, Friendship, I may say to thee,
    I love not to be there where chiders be.
Hypoc. No, God it knoweth, you are as full of honesty
    As a mary bone is full of honey.
    But sirrah, I pray you bid this gentleman welcome,   730
    For he is desirous in your company to come;
    I tell you, he is a man of the right making,
    And one that hath excellent learning;
    At his girdle he hath such a book
    That the popish priests dare not in him look.
    This is a fellow for the nonce.
Fellow. I love him the better, by Gog's precious bones;
    You are heartily welcome, as I may say;
    I shall desire you of better acquaintance,
    That of your company be bold I may.   740
    You may be sure if in me it lie,
    To do you pleasure you should it find,
    For by the mass I love you, both with heart and mind.
Juven. To say the same to you your gentleness doth me bind,
    And I thank you heartily for your kindness.
Hypoc. Will you see this gentleman's fineness,
    Your gentleness and your kindness?

116

I thank him, and I thank you,
And I think if the truth were sought,
The one bad and the other naught; 750
Never a good, I make God a vow.
But yet Fellowship tell me one thing,
Did you see little Bess this morning?
We should have our breakfast, yesternight she said,
But she hath forgotten it now, I am afraid.
Fellow. Her promise shall be performed and paid,
For I spake with her since the time I rose,
And then she told me how the matter goeth.
We must be with her between eight and nine,
And then her master and mistress will be at the preaching. 760
Juven. I purposed myself there to have been,
But this man provoked me to the contrary,
And told me that we should have merry company.
Fellow. Merry quod ha? We cannot choose but be merry,
For there is such a girl where as we go
Which will make us to be merry, whether we will or no.
Hypoc. The ground is the better on the which she doth go,
For she will make better cheer with that little which she
    can get,
Than many a one can with a great banquet of meat.
Juven. To be in her company my heart is set, 770
Therefore I pray you let us be gone.
Fellow. She will come for us herself anon,
For I told her before where we would stand,
And then she said she would beck us with her hand.
Juven. Now by the mass I perceive that she is a galland;
What, will she take pains to come for us hither?
Hypoc. Yea I warrant you, therefore you must be familiar
    with her.
When she cometh in place
You must her embrace
Somewhat handsomely, 780
Lest she think it danger
Because you are a stranger
To come in your company.
[*Juven.*] Yea by God's foot, that I will be busy;
And I may say to you, I can play the knave secretly.
                    [*Enter Abominable Living.*]

117

Abom. Liv. Hem, come away quickly,
　The back door is open; I dare not tarry.
　Come, Fellowship, come on away.
Hypoc. What, Unknown Honesty, a word:
　You shall not go yet, by God I swear. 790
　Here is none but your friends; you need not to fray
　Although this strange young gentleman be here.
Juven. I trust in me she will think no danger,
　For I love well the company of fair women.
Abom. Liv. Who you? Nay, ye are such a holy man,
　That to touch one ye dare not be bold.
　I think you would not kiss a young woman
　If one would give you twenty pound in gold.
Juven. Yes, by the mass, that I would;
　I could find in my heart to kiss you in your smock. 800
Abom. Liv. My back is broad enough to bear away that mock,
　For one hath told me many a time,
　That you have said, you would use no such wanton's
　　　company as mine.
Juven. By Gog's precious wounds, it was some whoreson villain!
　I will never eat meat that shall do me good
　Till I have cut his flesh, by Gog's precious blood;
　Tell me, I pray you, who it was,
　And I will trim the knave, by the blessed mass!
Abom. Liv. Tush, as for that do not you pass;
　That which I told you was but for love. 810
Hypoc. She did nothing else but prove
　Whether a little thing would you move
　To be angry and fret.
　What and if one had said so?
　Let such trifling matters go,
　And be good to men's flesh for all that.
Juven. To kiss her since she came I had clean forgot.
　　　　　　He kisseth.
　You are welcome to my company.
Abom. Liv. Sir, I thank you most heartily;
　By your kindness it doth appear. 820
Hypoc. What a hurly burly is here!
　Smick-smack and all this gear;
　You will to tick-tack I fear
　If you had time.

Well, wanton, well,
Iwis I can tell
That such smock smell
Will set your nose out of tune.

Abom. Liv. What man, you need not to fume;
Seeing he is come into my company now,   830
He is as well welcome as the best of you,
And if it lie in me to do him pleasure
He shall have it, you may be sure.

Fellow. Then old acquaintance is clean out of favour;
Lo Friendship, this gear goeth with a sleight.
He hath driven us twain out of conceit.

Hypoc. Out of conceit quod ha? No, no,
I dare well say she thinketh not so;
How say you, Unknown Honesty,
Do not you love Fellowship and me?   840

Abom. Liv. Yea, by the mass I love you all three,
But yet indeed, if I should say the truth,
Amongst all other, welcome, Master Youth.

Juven. Full greatly I do delight to kiss your pleasant mouth.

He kisseth.

I am not able your kindness to recompense;
I long to talk with you secretly, therefore let us go hence.

Abom. Liv. I agree to that, for I would not for twenty pence
That it were known where I have been.

Hypoc. What and it were known? It is no deadly sin;
As for my part I do not greatly care,   850
So that they find not your proper buttocks bare.

Abom. Liv. Now much fie upon you, how bawdy you are!
I wos, Friendship, it mought have been spoken at twice;
What think you for your saying that the people will surmise?

Juven. Who dare be so bold us to despise?
And if I may hear a knave speak one word,
I will run through his cheeks with my sword!

Fellow. This is an earnest fellow of God's word.
See, I pray you, how he is disposed to fight.

Juven. Why should I not and if my cause be right?   860
What, and if a knave do me beguile
Shall I stand crouching like an owl?
No, no, then you might count me a very cow.
I know what belongeth to God's law as well as you.

Abom. Liv. Your wit therein greatly I do allow;
  For and if I were a man as you are,
  I would not stick to give a blow
  To teach other knaves to beware.
  I beshrew you twice and if you do spare,
  But lay load on the flesh whatsoever befall;   870
  You have strength enough to do it withal.
Fellow. Let us depart and if that we shall;
  Come on masters, we twain will go before.
Juven. Nay, nay, my friend, stop there.
  It is not you that shall have her away;
  She shall go with me and if she go today.
Hypoc. She will go with none of you, I dare well say;
  She will go with me before you both.
Abom. Liv. To forsake any of your company I would be very
  Therefore I will follow you all three.   loath,
Hypoc. Now I beshrew his heart that to that will not agree;   881
  But yet, because the time shall not seem very long,
  Or ere we depart let us have a merry song.

They sing as followeth.

     Why should not Youth fulfil his own mind
     As the course of nature doth him bind?
     Is not everything ordained to do his kind?
     Report me to you, report me to you.
        Do not the flowers spring fresh and gay,
     Pleasant and sweet in the month of May?
     And when their time cometh they fade away.   890
     Report me to you, report me to you.
        Be not the trees in winter bare?
     Like unto their kind, such they are,
     And when they spring their fruits declare.
     Report me to you, report me to you.
        What should Youth do with the fruits of age
     But live in pleasure in his passage?
     For when age cometh his lusts will swage.
     Report me to you, report me to you.
        Why should not Youth fulfil his own mind   900
     As the course of nature doth him bind? &c

They go Forth. Here entreth Good Counsel.

[*Good Coun.*] Oh merciful Lord, who can cease to lament,
Or keep his heart from continual mourning,
To see how Youth is fallen from thy word and testament,
And wholly inclined to abominable living.
He liveth nothing according to his professing,
But, alas, his life is to thy word abusion;
Except thy great mercy, to his utter confusion.
Oh where is now the godly conversation
Which should be among the professors of thy word?   910
Oh where may a man find now one faithful congregation
That is not infected with dissension or discord?
Or amongst whom are all vices utterly abhorred?
Oh where is the brotherly love between man and man?
We may lament the time our vice began.
Oh where is the peace and meekness, long suffering and
Which are the fruits of God's Holy Spirit?   temperance,
With whom is the flesh brought under obedience?
Or who readeth the Scripture to the intent to follow it?
Who useth not now covetousness and deceit?   920
Who giveth unto the poor that which is due?
I think in this world few that live now.
Oh where is the godly example that parents should give
Unto their young family, by godly and virtuous living?
Alas, how wickedly do they themselves live,
Without any fear of God or his righteous threatening.
They have no respect unto the dreadful reckoning
Which shall be required of us, when the Lord shall come
As a rightful judge at the Day of Doom.
Oh what a joyful sight was it for to see   930
When Youth began God's word to embrace!
Then he promised godly Knowledge and me
That from our instructions he would never turn his face;
But now he walketh, alas, in the ungodliest chase,
Heaping sin upon sin, vice upon vice:
He that liveth most ungodly is counted most wise.

Here entreth Juventus.

[*Juven.*] Who is here playing at the dice?
I heard one speak of sins and sice;
His words did me entice
Hither to come.   940

Good Coun. Ah Youth, Youth, whither dost thou run?
  Greatly I do bewail thy miserable estate;
  The terrible plagues which in God's law are written,
  Hang over thy head both early and late.
  Oh fleshly capernite, stubborn and obstinate,
  Thou haddest lever forsake Christ, thy saviour and king,
  Than thy fleshly swinish lusts and abominable living.
Juven. What, old whoreson, art thou a chiding?
  I will play a spurt. Why should I not?
  I set not a mite by thy checking;   950
  What hast thou to do and if I lose my coat?
  I will trill the bones while I have one groat,
  And when there is no more ink in the pen,
  I will make a shift as well as other men.
Good Coun. Then I perceive you have forgotten clean
  The promise that you made unto Knowledge and me;
  You said such fleshly fruits should not be seen,
  But to God's word your life should agree.
  Full true be the words of the prophet Osey:
  No verity nor knowledge of God is now in the land,   960
  But abominable vices hath gotten the upper hand.
Juven. Your mind therein I do well understand;
  You go about my living to despise,
  But you will not see the beams in your own eyes.
Good Coun. The Devil hath you deceived, which is the author
  And trapped you in his snare of wicked hypocrisy;   of lies,
  Therefore all that ever you do devise
  Is to maintain your fleshly liberty.
Juven. I marvel why you do thus reprove me;
  Wherein do I my life abuse?   970
Good Coun. Your whole conversation I may well accuse,
  As in my conscience just occasion I find;
  Therefore be not offended, although I express my mind.
Juven. By the mass, if thou tell not truth I will not be behind
  To touch you as well again.
Good Coun. For this thing most chiefly I do complain:
  Have you not professed the knowledge of Christ's gospel?
  And yet I think no more ungodliness doth reign
  In any wicked heathen, Turk, or infidel.
  Who can devise that sin or evil   980
  That you practise not from day to day?

Yea, and count it nothing but a jest or a play.
Alas, what wantonness remaineth in your flesh!
How desirous are you to accomplish your own will!
What pleasure and delight have you in wickedness!
How diligent are you your lusts to fulfil!
Saint Paul saith that you ought your fleshly lusts to kill,
But unto his teaching your life ye will not frame;
Therefore in vain you bear a Christian's name.
Read the fifth to the Galathians, and there you shall see   990
That the flesh rebelleth against the spirit,
And that your own flesh is your most utter enemy
If in your soul's health you do delight.
The time were too long now to recite
What whoredom, uncleanness, and filthy communication,
Is dispersed with Youth in every congregation.
To speak of pride, envy, and abominable oaths,
They are the common practices of Youth.
To avance your flesh you cut and jag your clothes,
And yet ye are a great gospeller in the mouth.   1000
What shall I say for this blaspheming the truth?
I will show you what Saint Paul doth declare
In his Epistle to the Hebrews and the tenth chapter:
For him, saith he, which doth willingly sin or consent,
After he hath received the knowledge of the verity,
Remaineth no more sacrifice, but a fearful looking for
     judgement,
And a terrible fire, which shall consume the adversary.
And Christ saith that this blasphemy
Shall never be pardoned nor forgiven,
In this world, nor in the world to come.   1010
Juven. Alas, alas, what have I wrought and done?
                    He lieth down.
Here in this place I will fall down, desperate
To ask for mercy now I know it is too late.
Alas, alas, that ever I was begat!
I would to God I had never been born.
All faithful men that behold this wretched state
May very justly laugh me to scorn;
They may say my time I have evil spent and worn,
Thus in my first age to work my own destruction.
In the eternal pains is my part and portion.   1020

Good Coun. Why Youth, art thou fallen into desperation?
  What man, pluck up thine heart, and rise;
  Although thou see nothing now but thy condemnation,
  Yet it may please God again to open thy eyes.
  Ah wretched creature, what dost thou surmise?
  Thinkest not that God's mercy doth exceed thy sin?
  Remember his merciful promises, and comfort thyself in him.
Juven. Oh sir, this state is so miserable the which I lie in,
  That my comfort and hope from me is separated;
  I would to God I had never been!   1030
  Woe worth the time that ever I was created.
Good Coun. Ah, fair vessel, unfaithful and faint-hearted,
  Dost thou think that God is so merciless,
  That when the sinner doth repent and is converted,
  That he will not fulfil his merciful promises?
Juven. Alas sir, I am in such heaviness
  That His promises I cannot remember.
Good Coun. In thy wickedness continue no lenger,
  But trust in the Lord without any fear
  And his Merciful Promises shall shortly appear.   1040
Juven. I would believe, if I might them hear,
  With all my heart, power, and mind.
Good Coun. The living God hath him hither assigned;
  Lo, where he cometh even here by,
  Therefore mark his sayings diligently.

Here entreth God's Merciful Promises.

[*God's Prom.*] The Lord by his prophet Ezekiel saith in this wise
    plainly,
  As in the thirty-third chapter it doth appear:
  Be converted oh ye children and turn unto me,
  And I shall remedy the cause of your departure.
  And also he saith in the eighteenth chapter: 1050
  I do not delight in a sinner's death,
  But that he should convert and live, thus the Lord saith.
Juven. Then must I give neither credit nor faith
  Unto Saint Paul's saying, which this man did allege?
God's Prom. Yes, you must credit them according unto
    knowledge,
  For Saint Paul speaketh of those which resist the truth by
  And so end their lives without repentance: violence,

Thus Saint Augustine doth them define.
If unto the Lord's word you do your ears incline,
And observe those things which he hath commanded,   1060
This sinful state in the which you have lien
Shall be forgotten and never more remembered.
And Christ himself in the gospel hath promised
That he which in him unfeignedly doth believe,
Although he were dead, yet shall he live.

Juven. These comfortable sayings doth me greatly move
To arise from this wretched place.   *He riseth.*

God's Prom. For me his mercy sake thou shalt obtain his grace,
And not for thine own deserts—this must thou know.
For my sake alone he shall receive solace;   1070
For my sake alone he will thee mercy show;
Therefore to him, as it is most due,
Give most hearty thanks with heart unfeigned,
Whose name for evermore be praised.

Good Coun. The prodigal son, as in Luke we read,
Which in vicious living his goods doth waste,
As soon as his living he had remembered,
To confess his wretchedness he was not aghast;
Wherefore his father lovingly him embraced
And was right joyful, the text saith plain,   1080
Because his son was returned again.

Juven. Oh sinful flesh, thy pleasures are but vain.
Now I find it true as the Scripture doth say;
Broad and pleasant is the path which leadeth unto pain,
But unto eternal life full narrow is the way.
He that is not led by God's Spirit surely goeth astray,
And all that ever he doth shall be clean abhorred,
Although he brag and boast never so much of God's word.
Oh subtle Satan, full deceitful is thy snare;
Who is able thy falsehead to disclose?   1090
What is the man that thou dost favour or spare,
And dost not tempt him eternal joys to lose?
Not one in the world, surely I suppose;
Therefore happy is the man which doth truly wait,
Always to refuse thy deceitful and crafty bait.
When I had thought to live most Christianly,
And followed the steps of Knowledge and Good Counsel,
Ere I was ware thou haddest deceived me

And brought me into the path which leadeth unto Hell;
And of an earnest professor of Christ's gospel 1100
Thou madest me an hypocrite, blind and pervert,
And from virtue unto vice thou hadst clean turned my heart.
First, by Hypocrisy thou diddest me move
The mortification of the flesh clean to forsake,
And wanton desires to embrace and love.
Alas, to think on it my heart doth yet quake!
Under the title of Friendship to me he spake,
And so to wicked Fellowship did me bring,
Which brought me clean to Abominable Living.
Thus, I say, Satan did me deceive 1110
And wrapped me in sin many a fold;
The steps of Good Counsel I did forsake and leave,
And forgot the words which before to me he told.
The fruits of a true Christian in me waxed cold;
I followed mine own lusts; the flesh I did not tame,
And had them in derision which would not do the same.
Yet it hath pleased God of his endless mercy,
To give me respite, my life to amend.
From the bottom of my heart I repent my iniquity;
I will walk in his laws unto my live's end. 1120
From his holy ordinance I will never descend,
But my whole delight shall be to live therein,
Utterly abhorring all filthiness and sin.
[All Chris]tian people which be here present
[May lear]n by me hypocrisy to know,
[With the] which the Devil, as with a poison most pestilent,
Daily seeketh all men to overthrow.
Credit not all things unto the outward show,
But try them with God's word, that squire and rule most
　　just,
Which never deceiveth them that in him put their trust. 1130
Let not flattering Friendship, nor yet wicked company,
Persuade you in no wise God's word to abuse,
But see that ye stand steadfastly unto the verity,
And according to the rule thereof your doings frame and use.
Neither kinred nor fellowship shall you excuse
When you shall appear before the judgement seat,
But your own secret conscience shall then give an audit.
All you that be young, whom I do now represent,

Set your delight both day and night on Christ's Testament.
If pleasure you tickle, be not fickle, and suddenly slide,   1140
But in God's fear everywhere see that you abide.
In your tender age seek for knowledge, and after wisdom run,
And in your old age, teach your family to do as you have
    done.
Your bodies subdue unto virtue, delight not in vanity;
Say not 'I am young, I shall live long', lest your days
    shortened be.
Do not incline to spend the time in wanton toys and nice,
For idleness doth increase much wickedness and vice.
Do not delay the time, and say 'my end is not near',
For with short warning, the Lord's coming shall suddenly
    appear.
God give us grace his word to embrace, and to live
    thereafter,   1150
That by the same His holy name may be praised ever.
Good Coun. Now let us make our supplications together
    For the prosperous estate of our noble and virtuous king,
    That in his godly proceedings he may still persevere,
    Which seeketh the glory of God above all other thing.
    Oh Lord, endue his heart with true understanding,
    And give him a prosperous life long over us to reign,
    To govern and rule his people as a worthy ca<ptain>
Juven. Also let us pray for all the nobility of this [realm],
    And namely for those whom his grace hath au[thorized]   1160
    To maintain the public wealth over us and them,
    That they may see his gracious acts published,
    And that they, being truly admonished
    By the complaint of them which are wrongfully oppressed,
    May seek a reformation and see it redressed.
Good Coun. Then shall this land enjoy great quietness and rest;
    And give unto God most hearty thanks therefore,
    To whom be honour, praise, and glory for evermore.

FINIS

Quod R. Wever.

An Enterlude Intituled

Like wil to like quod the Deuel to the Colier, ve-
ry godly and ful of plesant mirth. Wherin is declared not one-
ly what punishement followeth those that wil rather fol-
lowe licentious liuing, then to esteem & followe good
council: and what great benefits and commodi
ties they receiue that apply them vnto
vertuous liuing and good exercises.
Made by Vlpian Fulwel.

Fiue may easely play this enterlude.

The names of the players.

The Prologue			Hance,		
Tom Tospot	for		Vertuous life	for	
Hankin hangman	one		Godes promises	one	
Tom Colier			Cutbert cutpurs		
Lucifer			Philip Fleming		
Ralfe Roister	for		Pierce Pickpurs	for	
Good fame	one		Honour	another	
Seueritie					

Nichol newfangle the vice.

AN INTERLUDE ENTITLED LIKE WILL TO LIKE QUOD THE DEVIL TO THE COLLIER

The Prologue

Cicero in his book *De Amicitia* these words doth express,
Saying nothing is more desirous than like is unto like;
Whose words are most true and of a certainty doubtless,
For the virtuous do not the virtuous company mislike,
But the vicious do the virtuous company eschew,
And like will unto like, this is most true.

    It is not my meaning your ears for to weary
With harkening what is th'effect of our matter:
But our pretence is to move you to be merry,
Merrily to speak, meaning no man to flatter.   10
The name of this matter, as I said whilere,
Is Like Will to Like Quoth the Devil to the Collier.

    Sith pithy proverbs in our English tongue doth abound,
Our author thought good such a one for to choose
As may show good example, and mirth may eke be found,
But no lascivious toys he purposeth for to use:
Herein as it were in a glass see you may
The advancement of virtue, of vice the decay;

    To what ruin ruffians and roisters are brought,
You may here see of them the final end: 20
Begging is the best, though that end be naught,
But hanging is worse if they do not amend.
The virtuous life is brought to honour and dignity
And at the last to everlasting eternity.

    And because divers men of divers minds be,
Some do matters of mirth and pastime require,
Other some are delighted with matters of gravity;
To please all men is our author's chief desire,
Wherefore mirth with measure to sadness is annexed,
Desiring that none here at our matter will be perplexed.   30

    Thus as I said I will be short and brief,
Because from this dump you shall relieved be,
And the Devil with the Collier, the thief that seeks the thief,
Shall soon make you merry as shortly you shall see;

And sith mirth for sadness is a sauce most sweet,
Take mirth then with measure, that best sauceth it.

*Finis [Exit Prologue.] Here entreth Nichol Newfangle the Vice
laughing, and hath a knave of clubs in his hand which as soon
as he speaketh he offereth unto one of the men or boys standing by.*

N. New. Ha, ha, ha, ha, now like unto like, it will be none
Stoop gentle knave and take up your brother.   other;
Why, is it so? And is it even so indeed?
Why, then may I say God send us good speed.   40
And is everyone here so greatly unkind,
That I am no sooner out of sight but quite out of mind?
Marry, this will make a man even weep for woe
That on such a sudden no man will me know.
Sith men be so dangerous now at this day,
Yet are women kind worms I dare well say.
How say you, woman? You that stand in the angle,
Were you never acquainted with Nichol Newfangle?
Then I see Nichol Newfangle is quite forgot,
Yet you will know me anon, I dare jeopard a groat.   50
Nichol Newfangle is my name, do you not me know?
My whole education to you I shall show.
For first before I was born I remember very well
That my grandsire and I made a journey into hell,
Where I was bound prentice before my nativity
To Lucifer himself, such was my agility.
All kind of sciences he taught unto me
That unto the maintenance of pride might best agree.
I learned to make gowns with long sleeves and wings,
I learned to make ruffs like calves' chitterlings,   60
Caps, hats, coats, and all kind of apparels,
And especially breeches as big as good barrels,
Shoes, boots, buskins, with many pretty toys,
All kind of garments for men, women, and boys.
Know you me now? I thought that at the last
All acquaintance from Nichol Newfangle is not past.
Nichol Newfangle was, and is, and ever shall be,
And there are but few that are not acquainted with me.
For so soon as my prenticehood was once come out,
I went by and by the whole world about.   70

Here the Devil entreth in but he speaketh not yet.

Sancte benedicite, whom have we here?
Tom Tumbler or else some dancing bear?
Body of me, it were best go no near:
For aught that I see it is my godfather Lucifer,
Whose prentice I have been this many a day:
But no mo words but mum, you shall hear what he will say.

This name Lucifer *must be written on his back and
in his breast.*

Luc. Ho, mine own boy, I am glad that thou art here.
N. New. He speaketh to you sir, I pray you come near.
Pointing to one standing by.
Luc. Nay, thou art even he of whom I am well apaid.
N. New. Then speak aloof off, for to come nie I am afraid. 80
Luc. Why so, my boy? As though thou didst never see me.
N. New. Yes godfather, but I am afraid it is now as oftentimes
    it is with thee:
For if my dame and thou hast been tumbling by the ears,
As oftentimes you do like a couple of great bears,
Thou carest not whom thou killest in thy raging mind.
Dost thou not remember since thou didst bruise me behind?
This hole in thy fury didst thou disclose,
That now may a tent be put in so big as thy nose.
This was when my dame called thee bottle-nosed knave;
But I am like to carry the mark to my grave. 90
Luc. Oh my good boy, be not afraid,
For no such thing hath happened as thou hast said;
But come to me my boy and bless thee I will,
And see that my precepts thou do fulfil.
N. New. Well godfather, if you will say aught to me in this case,
Speak, for in faith I mean not to kneel to that ill face.
If our Lady of Walsingham had no fairer nose and visage,
By the mass they were fools that would go to her on
Luc. Well boy, it shall not greatly skill   pilgrimage.
Whether thou stand or whether thou kneel. 100
Thou knowest what sciences I have thee taught,
Which are able to bring the world to naught;
For thou knowest that through pride from heaven I was cast
Even unto hell, wherefore see thou make haste
Such pride through new fashions in men's hearts to sow,
That those that use it may have the like overthrow.

From virtue procure men to set their minds aside,
And wholly employ it to all sin and pride.
Let thy new-fangled fashions bear such a sway,
That a rascal be so proud as he that best may.　　　　110

N. New. Tush, tush, that is already brought to pass,
For a very skipjack is prouder I swear by the mass,
And seeketh to go more gayer and more brave
Than doth a lord, though himself be a knave.

Luc. I can thee thank that so well thou hast played thy part:
Such as do so shall soon feel the smart.
Sith thou hast thus done there remaineth behind
That thou in another thing show thy right kind.

N. New. Then, good godfather, let me hear thy mind.

Luc. Thou knowest I am both proud and arrogant　　　120
And with the proud I will ever be conversant:
I cannot abide to see men that are vicious
Accompany themselves with such as be virtuous;
Wherefore my mind is, sith thou thy part canst play,
That thou adjoin like to like alway.

N. New. I never loved that well, I swear by this day.

Luc. What, my boy?

N. New. Your mind is, sith I fast three meals every Good
That I eat nothing but onions and leeks alway.　　　Friday,

Luc. Nay, my mind is, sith thou thy part canst play,　　　130
That thou adjoin like to like alway.

N. New. Tush, tush, godfather Devil, for that have thou no
care:
Thou knowest that 'like will to like' quoth the Devil to the
collier;
And thou shalt see that such match I shall make anon,
That thou shalt say I am thy good good sweet sweet godson.

Luc. I will give thee thanks when thou hast so done.

Here entreth in the Collier.

N. New. Well godfather, no mo words but mum,
For yonder comes the collier as seemeth me;
By the mass he will make a good mate for thee.
What, old acquaintance small remembrance?　　　140
Welcome to town, with a very vengeance.
Now welcome Tom Collier, give me thy hand.
As very a knave as any in England.

T. Col. By mass, God a marcy my vreend Nichol.

N. New. By God and welcome, gentle Tom Lick-hole.

T. Col. Cham glad to zee thee merry my vreend Nichol:
And how dost nowadays good Nichol?

N. New. And nothing else but even plain Nichol?

T. Col. I pray thee tell me how dost, good vreend Lick-hole.

N. New. It is turned from Nichol to Lick-hole with Tom
Collier;   150
I say no more Tom, but hold thy nose there.

T. Col. Nay hold thy tongue Nichol till my nose doth come,
So thou shalt take part and I shall take some.

N. New. Well Tom Collier, let these things pass away;
Tell me what market thou hast made of thy coals today.

T. Col. To every bushel cha zold but three peck:
Lo, here be the empty zacks on my neck.
Cha beguiled the whoresons that of me ha' bought;
But to beguile me was their whole thought.

N. New. But hast thou no conscience in beguiling thy
neighbour?   160

T. Col. No, marry, so ich may gains vor my labour;
It is a common trade nowadays, this is plain,
To cut one another's throat for lucre and gain.
A small vault as the world is now brought to pass.

N. New. Thou art a good fellow, I swear by the mass;
As fit a companion for the Devil as may be:
Lo, godfather Devil, this fellow will I match with thee.

Luc. And good Tom Collier, thou art welcome to me.

He taketh him by the hand.

T. Col. God a marzy good Devil, cham glad of thy company.

Luc. Like will to like I see very well.   170

N. New. Godfather, wilt thou dance a little before thou go
home to hell?

Luc. I am content, so that Tom Collier do agree.

T. Col. I will never refuse, Devil, to dance with thee.

N. New. Then, godfather, name what the dance shall be.

Luc. 'Tom Collier of Croydon hath sold his coal.'

N. New. Why then, have at it by my father's soul.

*Nichol Newfangle must have a gittern or some other
instrument (if it may be): but if he have not they
must dance about the place all three, and sing this*

133

song that followeth—which must be done also although they have an instrument.

Tom Collier of Croydon hath sold his coals
   And made his market today:
And now he danceth with the Devil,
   For like will to like alway.   180
Wherefore let us rejoice and sing,
   Let us be merry and glad,
Sith that the collier and the Devil
   This match and dance hath made.
Now of this dance we make an end,
   With mirth and eke with joy:
The collier and the Devil will be
   Much like to like alway.

Finis.

N. New. A ha, marry, this is trim singing;
   I had not thought the Devil to be so cunning,   190
   And by the mass Tom Collier as good as he:
   I see that like with like will ever agree.
T. Col. Farewell master Devil, vor ich must be gone.

Exit.

Luc. When then, farewell my gentle friend Tom.
N. New. Farewell Tom Collier, a knave be thy comfort.
   How saist thou godfather, is not this trim sport?
Luc. Thou art mine own boy; my blessing thou shalt have.
N. New. By my troth godfather, that blessing I do not crave,
   But if you go your way I will do my diligence
   As well in your absence as in your presence.   200
Luc. But thou shalt salute me or I go, doubtless,
   That in thy doings thou maist have the better success:
   Wherefore kneel down and say after me—
N. New. When the Devil will have it so, it must needs so be:

He kneeleth down.

   What shall I say, bottle-nosed godfather, canst thou tell?
Luc. All hail, oh noble prince of Hell—
N. New. All my dame's cow's tails fell down in the well.
Luc. I will exalt thee above the clouds—
N. New. I will salt thee and hang thee in the shrouds.

Luc. Thou art the enhancer of my renown—   210
N. New. Thou art Hance, the hangman of Callice town.
Luc. To thee be honour alone—
N. New. To thee shall come our hobbling Joan.
Luc. Amen.
N. New. Amen.
Luc. Now farewell my boy, farewell heartily.
N. New. Is there never a knave here will keep the Devil
Farewell, godfather, for thou must go alone: company?
I pray thee come hither again anon.

Exit Lucifer.

Marry, here was a benediction of the Devil's good grace!   220
Body of me, I was so afraid I was like to bestench the place;
My buttocks made buttons of the new fashion,
While the whoreson Devil was making his salutation.
But by mass, I am so glad as ever was Madge mare
That the whoreson Devil is joined with the knave collier;
As fit a match as ever could be picked out.
What saist thou to it, Joan with the long snout?

Tom Tosspot cometh in with a feather in his hat.

But who comes yonder, puffing as hot as a black pudding?
I hold twenty pound it is a ruffian, if a goose go a gooding.
T. Tos. Gog's heart and his guts, is not this too bad?   230
Blood, wounds, and nails, it will make a man mad.
N. New. I warrant you, here is a lusty one, very brave;
I think anon he will swear himself a knave.
T. Tos. Many a mile have I ridden, and many a mile have I
Yet can I not find for me a fit companion.   gone,
Many there be which my company would frequent,
If to do as they do I would be content.
They would have me leave off my pride and my swearing,
My new-fangled fashions, and leave off this wearing;
But rather than I such companions will have,
I will see a thousand of them laid in their grave.   240
Similis similem sibi quaerit; such a one do I seek
As unto myself in every condition is like.
N. New. Sir, you are welcome; ye seem to be an honest man,
And I will help you in this matter as much as I can:
If you will tarry here awhile, I tell you in good sooth,

I will find one as fit for you as a pudding for a friar's mouth.

T. Tos. I thank you, my friend, for your gentle offer to me;
I pray you tell me what your name may be.

N. New. Methink by your apparel you have had me in regard;
I pray you, of Nichol Newfangle have you never heard?   250

T. Tos. Nichol Newfangle? Why, we are of old acquaintance.

N. New. By my troth, your name is quite out of my
remembrance.

T. Tos. At your first coming into England, well I wot,
You were very well acquainted with Tom Tosspot.

N. New. Tom Tosspot? *Sancti amen,* how you were out of my
mind!

T. Tos. You know when you brought into England this new-
fangled kind,
That tosspots and ruffians with you were first acquainted.

N. New. It is even so, Tom Tosspot, as thou hast said.

T. Tos. It is an old saying that mountains and hills never meet,
But I see that men shall meet though they do not seek;   260
And I promise you, more joy in my heart I have found
Than if I had gained an hundred pound.

N. New. And I am as glad as one had given me a groat
That I have met now with thee, Tom Tosspot;
And seeing that thou wouldst a mate so fain have,
I will join thee with one that shall be as very a knave
As thou art thyself, thou may'st believe me.
Thou shalt see anon what I will do for thee,
For you seek for as very a knave as you yourself are:
For like will to like, quoth the Devil to the collier.   270

T. Tos. Indeed Nichol Newfangle, ye say the verity,
For like will to like, it will none other wise be.

Here entreth Rafe Roister.

N. New. Behold, Tom Tosspot, even in pudding time,
Yonder cometh Rafe Roister, an old friend of mine.
By the mass, for thee he is so fit a mate
As Tom and Tib for Kit and Kate.
Now welcome, my friend Rafe Roister, by the mass.

R. Rois. And I am glad to see thee here in this place.

N. New. Bid him welcome. Hark, he can play a knave's part.

T. Tos. My friend, you are welcome with all my heart.   280

R. Rois. God a mercy, good fellow, tell me what thou art.

N. New. As very a knave as thou, though the best be too bad.

T. Tos. I am one which of your company would be very glad.

R. Rois. And I will not your company refuse, of a certainty,
So that to my conditions your manners do agree.

T. Tos. It should appear by our sayings that we are of one
    mind,
For I know that roisters and tosspots come of one kind;
And as our names be much of one accord and much like
So I think our conditions be not far unlike.

R. Rois. If your name to me you will declare and show,   290
You may in this matter my mind the sooner know.

T. Tos. Few words are best among friends, this is true,
Wherefore I shall briefly show my name unto you.
Tom Tosspot it is, it need not to be painted,
Wherefore I with Rafe Roister must needs be acquainted.

N. New. In faith, Rafe Roister, if thou wilt be ruled by me,
We will dance hand in hand like knaves all three.
It is as unpossible for thee his company to deny,
As it is for a camel to creep through a needle's eye;
Therefore bid him welcome, like a knave as thou art.   300

R. Rois. By my troth Tom Tosspot, you are welcome with all
    my heart.

T. Tos. I thank you that my acquaintance ye will take in good
And by my troth I will be your sworn brother.   part,

N. New. Tush, like will to like, it will be none other,
For the virtuous will always virtuous company seek out;
A gentleman never seeketh the company of a lout,
And roisters and ruffians do sober company eschew:
For like will ever to like, this is most true.

R. Rois. Now friend Tom Tosspot, seeing that we are brethern
    sworn,
And neither of our companies from other may be forborne,   310
The whole trade of my life to thee I will declare.

T. Tos. And to tell you my property also I shall not spare.

N. New. Then my masters, if you will awhile abide it
Ye shall see two such knaves so lively described,
That if hell should be raked even by and by indeed,
Such another couple cannot be found, I swear by my creed.
Go to, sirs, say on your whole minds,
And I shall paint you out in your right kinds.
First Tom Tosspot, plead thou thy cause and thy name,

And I will sit in this chair and give sentence on the same;　　320
I will play the judge and in this matter give judgement.
How say you, my masters, are you not so content?
R. Rois. By my troth, for my part thereto I do agree.
T. Tos. I were to blame if any fault should be in me.
N. New. Then that I be in office neither of you do grudge?
Both. No indeed.
N. New. Where learned you to stand capped before a judge?
You souterly knaves, show you all your manners at once?
R. Rois. Why Nichol, all we are content.
N. New. And am I plain Nichol? And yet it is in my
　　arbitrement　　330
To judge which of you two is the verier knave;
I am master Nichol Newfangle, both gay and brave:
For seeing you make me your judge, I trow
I shall teach you both your liripup to know.
　　　　　　　　　He fighteth.
T. Tos. Stay yourself, sir, I pray you heartily.
R. Rois. I pray you be content and we will be more mannerly.
N. New. Nay, I cannot put up such an injury;
For seeing I am in office I will be known therefore:
Fend your heads, sirs, for I will to it once more.
　　　　　　　　He fighteth again.
R. Rois. I pray you be content, good gentle master Nichol.　　340
T. Tos. I never saw the like, by Gog's soul.
N. New. Well, my masters, because you do intend
To learn good manners, and your conditions to amend,
I will have but one fit more and so make an end.
　　　　　　　　He fighteth again.
R. Rois. I pray you sir, let us no more contend.
N. New. Marry, this hath breathed me very well;
Now let me hear how your tales ye can tell,
And I, master Judge, will so bring to pass
That I will judge who shall be knave of clubs at Christmas.
T. Tos. Gog's wounds, I am like *Phalaris* that made a Bull of
　　brass—　　350
N. New. Thou art like a false knave now, and evermore was.
T. Tos. Nay, I am like *Phalaris* that made a Bull of brass,
As a cruel torment for such as did offend;
And he himself first therein put was;
Even so are we brought now to this end,

138

In ordaining him a judge who will be honoured as a God.
So for our own tails we have made a rod.

R. Rois. And I am served as *Haman*, that prepared—

N. New. How was he served, I pray thee do me tell?

R. Rois. Who I speak of thou knowest not well.   360

N. New. Thou art served as Harry Hangman, captain of the
black guard.

R. Rois. Nay, I am served as *Haman* that prepared
A high pair of gallows for *Mardocheus* the Jew,
And was the first himself that thereon was hanged.
So I feel the smart of mine own rod, this is true;
But hereafter I will learn to be wise,
And ere I leap once I will look twice.

N. New. Well, Tom Tosspot, first let me hear thee:
How canst thou prove thyself a verier knave than he?

T. Tos. You know that Tom Tosspot men do me call—   370

N. New. A knave thou hast always been and evermore shall.

T. Tos. My conditions I am sure ye know as well as I—

N. New. A knave thou was born and so thou shalt die.

T. Tos. But that you are a judge, I would say unto you
Knaves are Christian men, else you were a Jew.

N. New. He calls me knave by craft, do you not see?
Sirrah, I will remember it when you think not on me.
Well, say what thou canst for thine own behoof:
If thou provest thyself the verier knave by good proof,
Thou must be the elder brother and have the patrimony;   380
And when he hath said, then do thou reply.
Even Thomas a Waterings or Tyburn Hill
To the falsest thief of you both, by my father's will.

R. Rois. I pray you sir, what is that patrimony?

N. New. I pray you leave your courtesy, and I will tell you by
and by.
If he be the more knave, the patrimony he must have,
But thou shalt have it if thou prove thyself the verier knave.
A piece of ground it is, that of Beggars' Manor do hold,
And whoso deserves it shall have it, ye may be bold,
Called Saint Thomas a Waterings or else Tyburn Hill,   390
Given and so bequeathed to the falsest knave by will.

T. Tos. Then I trow I am he that this patrimony shall possess,
For I, Tom Tosspot, do use this trade doubtless.
For morning till night I sit tossing the black bowl,

Then come I home and pray for my father's soul,
Saying my prayers with wounds, blood, guts, and heart,
Swearing and staring thus play I my part.
If any poor man have in a whole week earned one groat,
He shall spend it in one hour in tossing the pot.
I use to call servants and poor men to my company   400
And make them spend all they have unthriftily,
So that my company they think to be so good
That in short space their hair grows through their hood.
N. New. But will no gossips keep thee company now and than?
T. Tos. Tush, I am acquainted with many a woman
That with me will sit in every house and place;
But then their husbands had need fend their face,
For when they come home they will not be afeard
To shake the goodman, and sometime shave his beard.
And as for Flemish servants, I have such a train   410
That will quass and carouse, and therein spend their gain.
From week to week I have all this company,
Wherefore I am worthy to have the patrimony.
N. New. Thus thou may'st be called a knave in grain;
And where knaves are scant thou shalt go for twain.
But now, Rafe Roister, let me hear what thou canst say.
R. Rois. You know that Rafe Roister I am called alway,
And my conditions in knavery so far doth surmount
That to have this patrimony I make mine account;
For I entice young gentlemen all virtue to eschew   420
And to give themselves to riotousness, this is true.
Servingmen also by me are so seduced
That all in bravery their minds are confused;
Then if they have not themselves to maintain,
To pick and to steal they must be fain.
And I may say to you, I have such a train
That sometime I pitch a field on Salisbury plain;
And much more, if need were, I could say verily,
Wherefore I am worthy to have the patrimony.
N. New. He that shall judge this matter had need have more
    wit than I,   430
But seeing you have referred it unto my arbitrement,
In faith, I will give such equal judgement
That both of you shall be well pleased and content.
R. Rois. Nay, I have not done, for I can say much more.

N. New. Well, I will not have you contend any more:
But this farm which to beggars' manor doth appertain
I will equally divide between you twain.
Are you not content that so it shall be?
Both. As it pleaseth you, so shall we agree.
N. New. Then see that anon ye come both unto me.   440
R. Rois. Sir, for my part, I thank you heartily.
I promised of late to come unto a company
Which at Hob Filcher's for me do remain:
God be with you and anon I will come again.
T. Tos. Farewell brother Rafe, I will come to you anon.
N. New. Come again for you shall not so suddenly be gone:
See ye not who comes yonder? An old friend of yours,
One that is ready to quass at all hours.

> *Here entreth Hance with a pot and singeth as followeth.*
> *He singeth the first two lines and speaketh the rest as*
> *stammeringly as may be.*

Quass in heart and quass again and quass about the house a,
And toss the black bowl to and fro, and I brinks them all
    carouse a.   450
Hance. Be go go Gog's nowns ch ch cha drunk zo zo much
    today,
That be be mass ch cham a most drunk ich da da dare zay.
Chud spe spe spend a goo goo good groat
Tha that ich could vi vind my ca ca captain to to Tom
    Tosspot.
N. New. Sit down, good Hance, lest thou lie on the ground.
> *He setteth him in the chair.*
He knoweth not Tom Tosspot, I dare jeopard twenty pound.
T. Tos. He will know me by and by, I hold you a crown.
How dost thou servant Hance? How comes this to pass?
Hance. Ma ma master to to Tom, ch ch cham glad by by mass;
Ca ca carouse to to to thee go go good Tom.   460
> *He drinketh.*
N. New. Hold up good Hance, I will pledge thee anon.
R. Rois. Well, there is no remedy but I must be gone.
Hance. Ta ta tarry good vellow, a wo wo word or twain:
If tho tho thou thyself do do do not come again,
Bi bi bid Philip Fleming cu cu come hither to me,
Vo vo vor he must lead me home now ich do zee.

R. Rois. Then farewell Hance, I will remember thy arrant:
   He will be here by and by, I dare be his warrant.

Exit Rafe Roister.

N. New. Farewell Rafe Roister, with all my heart:
   Come anon and I will deliver thee thy part.   470
T. Tos. Now Hance, right now thou drank'st to me;
   Drink again and I will pledge thee.
Hance. Omni po po po tenti, all the po po pot is empty.
N. New. Why Hance, thou hast Latin in thy belly methink;
   I thought there was no room for Latin, there is so much drink.
Hance. Ich le le learned zome la la Latin when ich was a la la
   Ich ca ca can zay *Tu es nebulo*, ich learned of my dad,   lad;
   And ich could once he he help the p p priest to to zay mass;
   By gis ma man ich ha' been co co cunning when 'twas.
T. Tos. I knew Hance when he was as he saith,   480
   For he was once a scholar in good faith;
   But through my company he was withdrawn from thence,
   Through his riot and excessive expense,
   Unto this trade, which now you do in him see,
   So that now he is wholly addicted to follow me;
   And one of my guard he is now become.
   Well, Hance, well, thou wast once a white son.
N. New. Now, so God help me, thou art a pretty fellow Hance,
   A clean-legged gentleman, and as proper a paunch,
   As any I know between this and France.   490
Hance. Yes by by by God ich could once dance.
N. New. I speak of no dancing, little-bellied Hance,
   But seeing thou saist thou canst so well dance,
   Let me see whe'er thou canst dance lively.
Hance. Tha tha that ca ca can I do vull trimly.

*He danceth as evil-favoured as may be devised, and
in the dancing he falleth down, and when he riseth
he must groan.*

N. New. Rise again, Hance, thou had'st almost got a fall:
   But thou dancest trimly, legs and all.
   Body of me Hance, how doth thy belly canst thou tell?
   By the mass he hath berayed his breeches, methink by the
T. Tos. I will help thee up, Hance; give me thy hand.   smell. 500

He riseth.

Hance. By by mass ch ch chwas almost down I think ve verily.
N. New. Wast thou almost down, Hance? Marry, so think I;
  But thou art sick methink by thy groaning.
  He grunts like a bear when he is a moaning;
  Hark how his head aches, and how his pulses do beat.
  I think he will be hanged, his belly is so great.
Hance. Go go God a mercy good Tom, with all my heart.
N. New. If thou canst not leap Hance, let me see thee drink a
  And get thee out abroad into the air.   quart,
T. Tos. Tush, he had more need to sleep in this chair: 510
  Sit down, Hance, and thou shalt see anon
  Philip Fleming will come to fetch thee home.

> *Hance sitteth in the chair, and snorteth as though*
> *he were fast asleep.*

N. New. I pray thee Tom Tosspot, is this one of thy men?
T. Tos. He is a companion of mine now and then.
N. New. By the faith of my body, 'such Carpenter such chips',
  And as the wise man said, 'such lettuce such lips':
  For 'like master like man', 'like tutor like scholar',
  And 'like will to like', quoth the Devil to the collier.
T. Tos. It is no remedy for it must needs so be:
  Like will to like, you may believe me.   520

> *Philip Fleming entreth with a pot in his hand.*

N. New. Lo where Philip Fleming cometh, even in pudding
  time.
T. Tos. He bringeth in his hand either good ale or else good
  wine.

> *Philip Fleming singeth these four lines following.*

  Troll the bowl and drink to me, and troll the bowl again,
  And put a brown toast in the pot for Philip Fleming's brain,
  And I shall toss it to and fro, even round about the house a,
  Good hostess now let it be so, I brinks them all carouse a.

P. Flem. Marry, here is a pot of noppy good ale,
  As clear as crystal, pure and stale;
  Now a crab in the fire were worth a good groat,
  That I might quass with my captain Tom Tosspot.   530
  What? I can no sooner wish, but by and by I have;
  God save mine eyesight, methink I see a knave.

What, captain, how goeth the world with you?

N. New. Why now I see the old proverb to be true:
Like will to like, both with Christian, Turk, and Jew.

T. Tos. Marry, Philip, even as I was wont to do.

P. Flem. Rafe Roister told me that I should find Hance here;
Where is he that he doth not appear?

N. New. I hold twenty pound the knave is blind.
Turn about, Philip Fleming, and look behind: 540
Hast thou drunk so much that thy eyes be out?
Lo, how he snoreth like a lazy lout.
Go to him, for he sleepeth sound;
Two such paunches in all England can scant be found.

P. Flem. Why Hance, art thou in thy prayers so devoutly?
Awake, man, and we two will quass together stoutly.

Hance. Domine dominus noster:
Methink I cha spied three knaves on a cluster.

N. New. Stay awhile for he saith his *Pater noster.*

Hance. Sanctum benedicitum, what have I dreamed?   550
By Gog's nowns, chad thought ich had been in my bed.
Cha dreamed zuch a dream as thou wilt marvel to hear:
Methought ich was drowned in a barrel of beer,
And by and by the barrel was turned to a ship
Which, methought, the wind made lively to skip;
And ich did sail therein from Flanders to France.
At last, ich was brought hither among a sort of knaves by
    chance.

T. Tos. Lo, Hance, here is Philip Fleming come now;
We will go drink together now, how saist thou?

Hance. I pray thee good Vilip, now lead me away.   560

P. Flem. Give me thy hand, and I will thee stay.

T. Tos. How say you, master Nichol, will you keep us company?

N. New. Go before, master Lick-hole, and I will come by and
Mates matched together, depart you three;   by.
I will come after, you may believe me.

> *They three are gone together, and Nichol Newfangle*
> *remaineth behind, but he must not speak till they be*
> *within.*

N. New. Ha ha ha ha ha ha ha ha!
Now three knaves are gone, and I am left alone,
Myself here to solace.

Well done, gentle Joan, why begin you to moan?
Though they be gone I am in place.   570
    And now will I dance, now will I prance,
For why? I have none other work.
Snip, snap, butter is no bone meat,
Knaves' flesh is no pork.
    Hey tisty tosty, an owl is a bird,
Jackanapes hath an old face;
You may believe me at one bare word,
How like you this merry case?
    A piece of ground they think they have found:
I will tell you what it is;   580
For I them told of beggars' manor it did hold—
A staff and a wallet, iwis,
    Which in short space, even in this place
Of me they shall receive.
For when that their drift, hath spent all their thrift,
Their minds I shall deceive.
    I trow you shall see more knaves come to me,
Which whensoever they do
They shall have their meed as they deserve indeed,
As you shall see shortly these two.   590
    When they do pretend to have a good end
Mark well then what shall ensue;
A bag and a bottle, or else a rope knottle;
This shall they prove too true.
    But mark well this game, I see this gear frame—
Lo, who cometh now in such haste?
It is Cutbert Cutpurse and Pierce Pickpurse;
Give room now a little cast.

> *Here entreth Cutbert Cutpurse and Pierce Pickpurse.*
> *Cutbert Cutpurse must have in his hand a purse of*
> *money or counters in it, and a knife in one hand*
> *and a whetstone in the other; and Pierce must have*
> *money or counters in his hand and jingle it as he*
> *cometh in.*

C. *Cutp.* By Gog's wounds it doth me good to the heart
    To see how cleanly I played this part!   600
While they stood thrusting together in the throng,
I began to go them among,

145

And with this knife which here you do see,
I cut away this purse cleanly.

N. New. See to your purses my masters, and be ruled by me,
For knaves are abroad; therefore beware:
You are warned; and ye take not heed I do not care.

P. Pick. And also, so soon as I had espied
A woman in the throng whose purse was fat,
It took it by the strings, and cleanly it untied;   610
She knew no more of it than Gib our cat.
Yet at the last she hied apace
And said that the money in my hand she saw:
'Thou whore,' said I, 'I will have an action of the case,
And seeing thou saist so I will try the law.'

C. Cutp. How saist thou, Pierce Pickpurse, art thou not agreed
These two booties equally to divide?

P. Pick. Then let us count the total sum
And divide it equally, when we have done.

N. New. My masters, here is a good fellow that would fain
have some.   620

C. Cutp. What, Nichol Newfangle, be you here?
So God help me, I am glad with all my heart.

P. Pick. Then ere we depart we will have some cheer,
And of this booty you shall have your part.

N. New. I thank you both even heartily,
And I will do somewhat for you by and by.
Are not you two sworn brothers in every booty?

Both. Yes, that we are truly.

N. New. Then can I tell you news which you do not know;
Such news as will make you full glad, I trow.   630
But first tell me this, Pierce Pickpurse,
Whether is the elder, thou or Cutbert Cutpurse?

P. Pick. In faith, I think we are both of one age well nigh.

C. Cutp. I suppose there is no great difference truly;
But wherefore ask you, I pray you tell me why?

N. New. I will tell you the cause without any delay:
For a piece of land is fallen, as I hear say,
Which by succession must come to one of you;
A proper plot it is, this is most true.
For thou, Cutbert Cutpurse, wast Cutbert Cut-throat's son,   640
And thou, Pierce Pickpurse, by that time thou hast done,
Canst derive thy pedigree from an ancient house:

146

Thy father was Tom Thief and thy mother Tib Louse.
This piece of land, whereto you inheritors are,
Is called the Land of the Two-legged Mare,
In which piece of ground there is a mare indeed
Which is the quickest mare in England for speed.
Therefore, if you will come anon unto me
I will put you in possession, and that you shall see.

C. Cutp. I cannot believe that such luck is happened to us.　　　　650
N. New. It is true that I to you do discuss.
P. Pick. If you will help us to this piece of ground,
Both of us to you shall think ourselves bound.
N. New. Yes in faith, you shall have it, you may believe me;
I will be as good as my word, as shortly you shall see.
C. Cutp. Then, brother Pierce, we may think ourselves happy
That ever we were with him acquainted.
P. Pick. Even so we may, of a certainty,
That such good luck unto us hath happened.
But, brother Cutbert, is it not best　　　　　　　　　　　　660
To go in for a while and distribute this booty?
Where as we three will make some feast,
And quass together and be merry.
C. Cutp. What say you, Nichol? I do agree.

Here entreth in Virtuous Living.

N. New. But soft awhile, be ruled by me.
Look yonder a little, do you not see
Who cometh yonder? Awhile we will abide;
Let him say his pleasure and we will stand aside.
V. Liv. Oh gracious God, how wonderful are thy works;
How highly art thou of all men to be praised;　　　　　　　670
Of Christians, Saracens, Jews, and also Turks
Thy glory ought to be erected and raised.
What joys hast thou prepared for the virtuous life
And such as have thy name in love and in awe!
Thou hast promised salvation to man, child, and wife
That thy precepts observe and keep well thy law.
And to the virtuous life what doth ensue?
Virtutis premium honor, Tully doth say:
Honour is the guerdon for virtue due,
And eternal salvation at the latter day.　　　　　　　　　680
How clear in conscience is the virtuous life!

The vicious hath consciences so heavy as lead;
Their conscience and their doing is alway at strife,
And although they live, yet to sin they are dead.

N. New. God give you good morrow sir, how do you today?

V. Liv. God bless you also both now and alway.
I pray you, with me have you any acquaintance?

N. New. Yea, marry, I am an old friend of yours, perchance.

V. Liv. If it be so, I marvel very much
That the dullness of my wit should be such   690
That you should be altogether out of my memory:
Tell me your nane, I pray you heartily.

N. New. By the faith of my body you will appose me by and by.
But, in faith, I was but little when I was first born,
And my mother to tell me my name thought it scorn.

V. Liv. I will never acquaint me with such in any place
As are ashamed of their names, by God's grace.

N. New. I remember my name, now it is come to my mind;
I have mused much before I could it find:
Nichol Newfangle it is, I am your old friend.   700

V. Liv. My friend? Marry, I do thee defy,
And all such company I do deny;
For thou art a companion for roisters and ruffians,
And not fit for any virtuous companions.

N. New. And, in faith, art thou at plain defiance?
Then I see I must go to mine old acquaintance.
Well, Cutbert Cutpurse and Pickpurse, we must go together,
For 'like will to like', quoth the Devil to the collier.

V. Liv. Indeed thou saist true, it must needs be so,
For like will ever to his like go;   710
And my conditions and thine so far do disagree
That no familiarity between us may be;
For thou nourishest vice, both day and night:
My name is Virtuous Life, and in virtue is my delight;
So vice and virtue cannot together be united,
But the one the other hath always spited:
For as water quencheth fire and the flame doth suppress,
So virtue hateth vice and seeketh a redress.

P. Pick. Tush, if he be so dangerous, let us not him esteem;
And he is not for our company, I see very well,   720
For if he be so holy as he doth seem,
We and he differ as much as Heaven and Hell.

148

C. Cutp. You know that like will to like alway,
    And you see how holily he is now bent.
    To seek his company why do we assay?
    I promise you, do you what you will, I do not consent,
    For I pass not for him be he better or be he worse.
N. New. Friend, if you be wise beware your purse,
    For this fellow may do you good when all comes to all,
    If you chance to lose your purse in Cutpurse Hall.   730
    But in faith fare ye well, sith of our company you be weary,
    We will go to a place where we will be merry,
    For I see your company and ours do far differ,
    For 'like will to like', quoth the Devil to the collier.
P. Pick. Well, let us be gone and bid him adieu,
    For I see this proverb proveth very true.
C. Cutp. Then let us go to Hob Filcher's house,
    Where we will be merry and quass carouse;
    And there shall we find Tom Tosspot with other mo
    Meet mates for us; therefore let us go.   740
N. New. Then seeing we are all of one mind,
    Let us three go, and leave a knave here behind.

They sing this song as they go out from the place.

C. Cutp. Good hostess lay a crab in the fire and broil a mess of
        souse a,
    That we may toss the bowl to and fro, and brinks them all
        carouse a;
N. New. And I will pledge Tom Tosspot till I be as drunk as a
        mouse a;
    Whoso will drink to me all day, I will pledge them all
        carouse a.
P. Pick. Then we will not spare for any cost, so long as we be in
        house a;
    Then hostess fill the pot again, for I pledge them all
        carouse a.

Finis. Exeunt they three.

V. Liv. Oh wicked imps, that have such delight
    In evil conversation, wicked and abhominable,   750
    And from virtue's lore withdraw yourselves quite,
    And lean to vice most vile and detestable!
    How prone and ready we are vice to ensue;

How deaf we be good counsel to hear;
How strange we make it our hearts to renew;
How little we have God's threats in fear.

> *When this is spoken he must pause awhile, and*
> *then say as followeth.*

Saint Augustine saith in his fifth book *De Civitate Dei*,
Conjunctae sunt edes Virtutis et Honoris, saith he;
The houses of Virtue and Honour joined together be,
And so the way to Honour's house is disposed   760
That through Virtue's house he must needs pass,
Or else from honour he shall soon be deposed,
And brought to that point that he before was.
　But if through virtue honour be attained,
　The path to salvation may soon be gained.
Some there be that do fortune prefer;
Some esteem pleasure more than virtuous life;
But in my opinion all such do err,
For virtue and fortune be not at strife.
　Where virtue is, fortune must needs grow,   770
　But fortune without virtue hath soon the overthrow.
Thrice happy are they that do virtue embrace,
For a crown of glory shall be their reward;
Satan at no time may him anything deface,
For God over him will have such regard
　That his foes he shall soon tread underfoot,
　And by God's permission pluck them up by the root.
It booteth not vice against virtue to stir;
For why? Vice is feeble and of no force,
But *Virtus eterna preclaraque habetur*;   780
Wherefore I would all men would have remorse
　And eschew evil company vile and pernicious,
　Delight in virtuous men, and hate the vicious.
And as the end of virtue is honour and felicity,
So mark well the end of wickedness and vice—
Shame in this world and pain eternally;
Wherefore you that are here, learn to be wise,
　And the end of the one with the other weigh
　By that time you have heard the end of this play.
But why do I thus much say in the praise of virtue,   790
Sith the thing praiseworthy needs no praise at all?

150

It praiseth itself sufficiently, this is true,
Which chaseth away sin as bitter as gall;
    And where virtue is, it need not to be praised,
    For the renown thereof shall soon be raised.

Intrat Good Fame.

G. Fame. Oh Virtuous Life, God rest you merry;
    To you am I come for to attend.
V. Liv. Good Fame, you are welcome heartily.
    I pray you, who did you hither send?
G. Fame. Even God's Promise hath sent me unto you,   800
    Willing me from you not to depart,
    But always to give attendance due
    And in no wise from you to start;
    For God of his promise hath most liberally
    Sent me, Good Fame, to you, Virtuous Life,
    Whereby it may be seen manifestly,
    God's great zeal to virtue, both in man and wife.
    For why? They may be sure that I, Good Fame,
    From the virtuous life will never stray;
    Whereby honour and renown may grow to their name,   810
    And eternal salvation at the latter day.
V. Liv. God is gracious and full of great mercy
    To such as in virtue set their whole delight,
    Pouring his benefits on them abundantly.
    Oh man, what meanest thou with thy Saviour to fight?
    Come unto him, for he is full of mercy,
    The fountain of virtue and of godliness the spring;
    Come unto him and thou shalt live everlastingly;
    He doth not require thee any price to bring.
    Venite ad me omnes qui laboratis et onerati   820
    estis et ego resossilabo vos.
    Come unto me ye that travail, saith he,
    And such as with sin are heavily loaden,
    And of me myself refreshed you shall be.
    Repent, repent, your sins shall be downtrodden.
    Well, Good Fame, sith God of his goodness
    Hath hither sent you on me to attend,
    Let us give thanks to him with humbleness,
    And persuade with all men their lives to amend.
G. Fame. Virtuous Life, I do thereto agree,   830

For it becometh all men for to do so.
But behold, yonder cometh God's Promise as seemeth me,
And Honour with him cometh also.

V. Liv. Such godly company pleaseth me very well,
For vicious men from our company we should expel.

Intrat God's Promise and Honour with him.

G. Prom. God rest you merry both, and God be your guide.

Hon. We are now come to the place where we must abide,
For from you, Virtuous Life, I Honour may not slide.

G. Prom. I am God's Promise, which is a thing eterne,
And nothing more surer than his promise may be;   840
A sure foundation to such as will learn
God's precepts to observe. Then must they needs see
Honour in this world and at last a crown of glory,
Ever in joy and mirth and never to be sorry.
Wherefore, oh Virtuous Life, to you we do repair
As messengers from God his promise to fulfil;
And therefore sit you down now in this chair
For to endue you with honour it is God's promise and will.

Virtuous Living sitteth down in the chair.

Hon. Now take this sword in hand as a token of victory;
This crown from my head to you I shall give;   850
I crown you with it as one most worthy,
And see that all vice ye do punish and grieve;
For in this world I, Honour, with you shall remain,
And Good Fame from you cannot refrain;
And after this life a greater crown you shall attain.

V. Liv. What heart can think, or what tongue can express
The great goodness of God which is almighty?
Who seeth this and seeks not vice to suppress?
Honour, Good Fame, yea, and life everlastingly?
Thy name be praised, oh Lord, therefore,   860
And to thee only be glory and honour.

G. Fame. Sith God's Promise hath brought Honour into place,
I will for a while leave you three alone,
For I must depart now for a little space,
But I shall come to you again anon.

Exit Good Fame.

V. Liv. God's Promise is infallible, his word is most true,

And to ground thereon a man may be bold,
As Scripture doth testify and declare unto you;
On which foundation your building you may behold.
    For virtuous rulers the fruit of felicity do reap,   870
    And reward of fame and honour to themselves they heap.
Hon. Seeing we have now endued him with the crown and the
    Which is due unto him by God's promise and word,   sword
    Let us three sing unto God with one accord.
G. Prom. To sing praises unto God it liketh well me.
V. Liv. And I also with you do thereto agree;
    A pleasant noise to God's ears it must needs bring
    That God's Promise, Honour, and Virtuous Life do sing.

They sing this song following.

Life is but short, hope not therein,   (*This must be sung*)
Virtue immortal seek for to win.   (*after every verse*)   880
    Whoso to virtue doth apply
Good Fame and Honour must obtain,
And also live eternally,
For Virtuous Life this is the gain.
    Life is but, etc.

God's Promise sure will never fail;
His holy word is a perfect ground:
The fort of virtue, oh man assail,
Where treasure always doth abound.
    Life is but, etc.   890

To thee alone be laud and praise
Oh Lord, that art so merciful:
Who never failed at all assays
To aid and help the pitiful.
    Life is but, etc.

Finis. Exeunt omnes.

*Here entreth in Nichol Newfangle, and bringeth in with him a bag, a staff,
a bottle, and two halters, going about the place showing it unto the audience
and singeth this:*

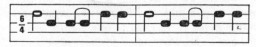

153

N. New. Trim merchandise trim trim, trim merchandise trim
    trim.

> (*He may sing this as oft as he thinketh good.*)

Marry, here is merchandise, whoso list for to buy any.
Come see for your love and buy for your money.
This is land which I must distribute anon
According to my promise, or I be gone.   900
For why? Tom Tosspot, since he went hence,
Hath increased a noble just unto nine pence;
And Rafe Roister, it may no other wise be chosen,
Hath brought a pack of wool to a fair pair of hosen.
This is good thrift sirs, learn it who shall.
And now a couple of fellows are come from Cutpurse Hall,
And there have they brought many a purse to wrack;
Lo, here is gear will make their necks for to crack.
For I promised Tom Tosspot and Rafe Roister a piece of land,
Lo here it is, ready in my right hand—   910
A wallet and a bottle, but it is not to be sold;
It told them before that of Beggar's Manor it did hold.
And for Cutbert Cutpurse and Pierce Pickpurse here is good
    fare;
This is the Land of the Two-legged Mare
Which I to them promised, and divide it with discretion:
Shortly you shall see I will put them in possession.
How like you this merchandise, my masters? Is it not trim?
A wallet, a bottle, a staff, and a string:
How saist thou, Wat Waghalter, is not this a trim thing?
In faith, Rafe Roister is in good case as I suppose,   920
For he hath lost all that he hath, save his doublet and his
    hose,
And Tom Tosspot is even at that same point,
For he would lose a limb or jeopard a joint.
But behold, yonder they come both, now all is gone and
    spent;
I know their errand and what is their intent.

> *Here entreth in Rafe Roister and Tom Tosspot in*
> *their doublet and their hose, and no cap nor hat on*
> *their head saving a nightcap, because the strings of*
> *the beards may not be seen; and Rafe Roister must*
> *curse and ban as he cometh in.*

T. Tos. Well, be as be may is no banning,
    But I fear that when that this gear shall come to scanning,
    The land to the which we did wholly trust
    Shall be gone from us, and we cast in the dust.

R. Rois. Gog's blood, if Nichol Newfangle serve us so   930
    We may say that we have had a shrewd blow,
    For all that I had is now lost at the dice;
    My sword, my buckler, and all, at cinque and cise.
    My coat, my cloak, and my hat also,
    And now in my doublet and my hose I am fain to go.
    Therefore, If Nichol Newfangle help not now at a pinch
    I am undone, for of land I have not an inch.

T. Tos. By Gog's wounds, even so is it now with me;
    I am in my doublet and my hosen as you see,
    For all that I had doth lie at pledge for ale: 940
    By the mass I am as bare as my nail.
    Not a cross of money to bless me have I;
    But I trow we shall meet Nichol Newfangle by and by.

N. New. Turn hither, turn hither, I say, sir knave,
    For I am even he that you so fain would have.

R. Rois. What, Master Nichol? Are you here all this while?

N. New. I think I am here, or else I do thee beguile.

T. Tos. So God help me, I am glad that you be in sight,
    For in faith your presence hath made my heart light.

N. New. I will make it lighter anon, I trow: 950
    My masters, I have a piece of land for you, do you not know?

R. Rois. Marry, that is the cause of our hither resort,
    For now we are void of all joy and comfort.

T. Tos. You see in what case we now stand in,
    And you heard us also even now, I ween;
    Wherefore, good Master Nichol, let us have this land now,
    And we shall think ourselves much bound unto you.

N. New. You know that I this land must divide,
    Which I shall do—but a while abide;
    All thy goods for ale at pledge be,   960
    And thou saist a pair of dice have made thee free.
    First, Rafe Roister, come thou unto me;
    Because thou hast lost every whit at dice,
    Take thou this bag to carry bread and cheese;

             He giveth the bag to Rafe Roister, and
             the bottle to Tom Tosspot.

And take thou this bottle, and mark what I shall say;
If he chance to eat the bread and cheese by the way
Do thou in this matter follow my counsel;
Drink up the drink and knock him about the head with the
And because that Rafe is the elder knave,   bottle.
This staff also of me he shall have.   970
R. Rois. But where is the land that to us you promised?
N. New. In faith, good fellows, my promise is performed.
T. Tos. By Gog's blood, I thought that it would be so.
N. New. This must you have whether you will or no;
Or else fall to work with shovel and with spade,
For begging now must be your chiefest trade.
R. Rois. Gog's heart, can I 'way with this life?
To beg my bread from door to door?
I will rather cut my throat with a knife
Than I will live thus beggarly and poor.   980
By Gog's blood, rather than I will it assay
I will rob and steal, and keep the highway.
T. Tos. Well, Rafe Roister, seeing we be in this misery,
And labour we cannot, and to beg it is a shame;
Yet better it is to beg most shamefully
Than to be hanged, and to thievery ourselves frame.
N. New. Now, my masters, learn to beware;
But 'like will to like', quoth the Devil to the collier.
R. Rois. Oh Lord, why did not I consider before
What should of roisting be the final end?   990
Now the horse is stol'n, I shut the stable door;
Alas, that I had time my life to amend.
Time I have, I must needs confess,
But yet in misery that time must be spent,
Seeing that my life I would not redress,
But wholly in riot I have it all spent;
Wherefore I am now brought to this exigent.
But the time past cannot be called, this is no nay,
Wherefore all here take example by me.
Time tarrieth no man, but passeth still away;   1000
Take time while time is, for time doth flee.
Use well your youthly years, and to virtuous lore agree;
For if I to virtue had any respect
This misfortune to me could not have chanced,
But because unto vice I was a subject

To no good fame may I be now advanced.
My credit also is now quite stanched;
Wherefore I would all men my woeful case might see,
That I to them a mirror might be.
T. Tos. Oh all ye parents, to you I do say,　　　　　　1010
Have respect to your children and for their education,
Lest you answer therefore at the latter day,
And your meed shall be eternal damnation.
If my parents had brought me up in virtue and learning
I should not have had this shameful end,
But all licenciously was my upbringing;
Wherefore learn by me your faults to amend.
But neither in virtue, learning, or yet honest trade
Was I bred up my living for to get:
Therefore in misery my time away must fade.　　　　　1020
For vicious persons, behold now the net;
I am in the snare, I am caught with the gin,
And now it is too late: I cannot again begin.
N. New. This gear would have been seen to before,
But now, my masters, you are on the score.
Be packing, I say, and get you hence;
Learn to say, 'I pray good master give me ninepence'.
R. Rois. Thou, villain, art only the causer of this woe,
Therefore thou shalt have somewhat of me or ere I go.
T. Tos. Thou hast given me a bottle here,　　　　　　1030
But thou shalt drink first of it, be it ale or beer.

　　　　　*Rafe Roister beateth him with his staff, and Tom
　　　　　Tosspot with his bottle.*

R. Rois. Take this of me before I go hence.
T. Tos. Take that of me in part of recompense.
N. New. Now am I driven to play the master of fence.
Come no near me you knaves for your life,
Lest I stick you both with this wood knife.
Back I say! Back thou sturdy beggar!
Body of me, they have ta'en away my dagger.

　　　　　*They have him down and beat him, and he crieth
　　　　　for help.*

R. Rois. Now in faith, you whoreson, take heed I you advise,
How you do any more young men entice.　　　　　　1040

T. Tos. Now farewell, thou hast thy just meed.

R. Rois. Now we go a begging, God send us good speed.

> *Rafe Roister and Tom Tosspot go out, and Severity the
> Judge entreth; and Nichol Newfangle lieth on the ground
> groaning.*

Sev. That upright judgement without partiality,
  Be ministered duly to ill-doers and offenders,
  I am one whose name is Severity,
  Appointed a judge to suppress evil-doers.
    Not for hatred, nor yet for malice,
    But to advance virtue and suppress vice.
  Wherefore *Isidorus* these words doth say:
  Non est Iudex si in eo non est Iusticia   1050
  He is not a judge that justice doth want,
  But he that truth and equity doth plant.
    Tully also these words doth express,
    Which words are very true, doubtless:
  Semper iniquus est Iudex, qui aut invidet aut favet.
  They are unrightful judges all
  That are either envious or else partial.

N. New. Help me up, good sir, for I have got a fall.

Sev. What cause have you, my friend, thus heavily to groan?

N. New. Oh sir, I have good cause to make great moan.   1060
  Here were two fellows but right now
  That I think have killed me, I make God a vow.
  I pray you tell me, am I alive or am I dead?

Sev. Fellow, it is more meet for thee to be in thy bed
  Than to lie here in such sort as thou dost.

N. New. In faith, I should have laid some of the knaves in the
  If I had had your sword right now in presence;   dust,
  I would have had a leg or an arm ere they had gone hence.

Sev. Who is it that hath done thee this injury?

N. New. A couple of beggars have done me this villainy.   1070

Sev. I see if severity should not be executed
  One man should not live by another;
  If such injuries should not be confuted
  The child would regard neither father nor mother.
  Give me thy hand and I shall help thee.

N. New. Hold fast your sword then, I pray you heartily.
               He riseth.

Sev. Now friend, it appeareth unto me
    That you have been a traveller of the country,
    And such as travel do hear of things done,
    As well in the country as the City of London.   1080
    How say you, my friend, can you tell any news?
N. New. Than can I, for I came lately from the stews.
    There are knaves abroad, you may believe me,
    As in this place shortly you shall see.
    No more words but mum, and stand awhile aside;
    Yonder cometh two knaves, therefore abide.

Intrat Cutbert Cutpurse and Pierce Pickpurse.

C. Cutp. By Gog's wounds, if he help not now we are undone.
    By the mass, for my part I wot not whither to run;
    We be so pursued on every side
    That by Gog's heart I wot not where to abide.   1090
    Every constable is charged to make privy search,
    So that if we may be got, we shall be throwen over the perch.
P. Pick. If Nichol Newfangle help us not now in our need,
    We are like in our business full evil to speed;
    Therefore let us make no delay,
    But seek him out of hand and be gone away.
N. New. Soft my masters awhile, I you pray,
    For I am here for whom you do seek;
    For you know that like will never from like.
    I promised you of late a piece of land,   1100
    Which by and by shall fall into your hand.
C. Cutp. What, Master Nichol? How do you today?
P. Pick. For the passion of God, Master Nichol, help to rid us
        away,
    And help us to the land whereof you did say,
    That we might make money of it by and by,
    For out of the realm we purpose to flee.
N. New. Marry, I will help you I swear by All Hallows,
    And will not part from you till you come to the gallows.
    Lo, noble Severity, these be they without doubt
    On whom this rumour of thievery is gone about;   1110
    Therefore my masters, here is the snare
    That shall lead you to the Land called the Two-legged Mare.
        He putteth about each of their necks a halter.
Sev. My friend, hold them fast even in that plight.

159

N. New. Then come and help me with your sword, for I fear
   they will fight.
Sev. Strive not, my masters, for it shall not avail,
   But awhile give ear unto my counsail;
   Your own words hath condemned you for to die,
   Therefore to God make yourselves ready,
   And by and by I will send one, which for your abusion
   Shall lead you to the place of execution.   1120
N. New. Help to tie their hands before ye be gone.
          He helpeth to tie them.
Sev. Now they are bound, I will send one to you anon.

          Exit.

N. New. Ah, my masters, how like you this play?
   You shall take possession of your land today;
   I will help to bridle the two-legged mare,
   And both you for to ride need not to spare.
   Now, so God help me, I swear by this bread,
   I marvel who shall play the knave when you twain be dead.
C. Cutp. Oh cursed caitiff, born in an evil hour,
   Woe unto me that ever I did thee know,   1130
   For of all iniquity thou art the bower;
   The seed of Satan thou dost always sow;
   Thou only hast given me the overthrow.
   Woe worth the hour wherein I was born,
   Woe worth the time that ever I knew thee,
   For now in misery I am forlorn.
   Oh all youth, take example by me;
   Flee from evil company as from a serpent you would flee,
   For I to you all a mirror may be.
   I have been daintily and delicately bred,   1140
   But nothing at all in virtuous lore,
   And now I am but a man dead;
   Hanged I must be, which grieveth me full sore;
   Note well the end of me therefore.
   And you that fathers and mothers be,
   Bring not up your children in too much liberty.
P. Pick. Sith that by the law we are now condemned,
   Let us call to God for his mercy and his grace,
   And exhort that all vice may be amended,
   While we in this world have time and space;   1150

And though our lives have licenciously been spent,
Yet at the last to God let us call,
For he heareth such as are ready to repent,
And desireth not that sinners should fall.
Now are we ready to suffer, come when it shall.

Here entreth in Hankin Hangman.

N. New. Come, Hankin Hangman, let us two cast lots
    And between us divide a couple of coats.
    Take thou the one and the other shall be mine;
    Come, Hankin Hangman, thou cam'st in good time.
        They take off the coats and divide them.
H. Hang. Thou should'st have one, Nichol, I swear by the
    For thou bringest work for me daily to pass,   mass,   1160
    And through thy means I get more coats in one year
    Than all my living is worth beside, I swear;
    Therefore, Nichol Newfangle, we will depart never,
    For 'like will to like', quoth the Devil to the collier.
N. New. Now farewell, Hankin Hangman, farewell to thee.
H. Hang. Farewell, Nichol Newfangle. Come you two with me.

      Hankin goeth out and leadeth the one in his right
      hand and the other in his left, having halters
      about their necks.

N. New. Ha, ha, ha, there is a brace of hounds, well worth a
    Behold the huntsman leadeth away;   dozen crowns,
I think in twenty towns, on hills and eke on downs,   1170
    They taken have their prey.
So well-liked was their hunting, on hill and eke on mountain,
    That now they be up in a leace:
To keep within a string, is it not a gay thing?
    Do all you hold your peace?
Why then, good gentle boy, how likest thou this play?
    No more but say thy mind;
I swear by this day, if thou wilt this assay,
    I will to thee be kind.
This is well brought to pass of me, I swear by the mass,   1180
    Some to hang and other some to beg;
I would I had Balaam's ass, to carry me where I was,
    How say you, little Meg?
Rafe Roister and Tom Tosspot are now not worth a groat,

So well with them it is:
I would I had a pot, for now I am so hot
  By the mass, I must go piss.
Philip Fleming and Hance, have danced a pretty dance,
  That all is now spent out;
And now a great mischance came on while they did prance; 1190
  They lie sick of the gout,
And in a spital house with little Lawrence Louse
  They be fain for to dwell;
If they eat a morsel of souse, or else a roasted mouse,
  They think they do fare well.
But as for Peter Pickpurse, and also Cutbert Cutpurse,
  You saw them both right now:
With them it is much worse, for they do ban and curse,
  For the halter shall them bow.
Now if I had my nag, to see the world wag 1200
  I would straight ride about:
Ginks do fill the bag; I would not pass a rag
  To hit you on the snout.

The Devil entreth.

Luc. Ho, ho, ho, mine own boy, make no more delay,
  But leap up on my back straightway.
N. New. Then who shall hold my stirrup while I go to horse?
Luc. Tush, for that do thou not force;
  Leap up I say, leap up quickly.
N. New. Woah, ball, woah, and I will come by and by.
  Now for a pair of spurs I would give a good groat, 1210
  To try whether this jade do amble or trot.
  Farewell my masters, till I come again,
  For now I must make a journey into Spain.

  He rideth away on the Devil's back. Here entreth
  Virtuous Life and Honour.

V. Liv. Oh worthy diadem, oh jewel most precious,
  Oh virtue, which dost all worldly things excel,
  How worthy a treasure thou art to the virtuous!
  Thy praise no pen may write nor no tongue tell;
  For I, who am called Virtuous Life,
  Have in this world both honour and dignity;
  Immortal fame of man, child, and wife, 1220

Daily waiteth and attendeth on me.
The commodity of virtue in me you may behold;
The enormity of vice you have also seen:
Therefore now to make an end we may be bold,
And pray for our noble and gracious queen.
Hon. To do so, Virtuous Life, it is our bounden duty,
And because we must do so before we do end,
To aid us therein Good Fame cometh verily,
Which daily and hourly on you doth attend.

Here entreth Good Fame.

G. Fame. Virtuous Life, do what you list;   1230
To pray or to sing I will you assist.
V. Liv. Oh Lord of hosts, oh King almighty,
Pour down thy grace upon our noble Queen;
Vanquish her foes, Lord, that daily and nightly
Through her thy laws may be sincerely seen.
Hon. The honourable Council also, oh Lord, preserve;
The Lords both of the clergy and of the temporality.
Grant that with meekness they may thee serve,
Submitting to thee with all humility.
G. Fame. Oh Lord, preserve the commons of this realm also; 1240
Pour upon them thy heavenly grace
To advance virtue and vice to overthrow,
That at last in Heaven with thee they may have place.

AMEN

FINIS qd. ULPIAN FULWELL

A SONG

Where like to like is matched so
That virtue must of force decay,
There God with vengeance, plagues, and woe,
By judgement just must needs repay.
   For like to like, the worldlings cry,
   Although both likes do grace defy.

And whereas Satan planted hath
In vicious minds a sinful trade;
There like to like do walk his path

163

By which to him like they are made.
  So like with like reward obtain,
  To have their meed in endless pain.

Likewise in faith where matches be,
And where as God hath planted grace,
There do his children still agree,
And like to like do run their race.
  Like Christ, like hearts of Christian men,
  As like to like well-coupled then.

Therefore like grace, like faith, and love,
Like virtue springs in each degree;
Where like assistance from above
Doth make them like so right to be.
  A holy God, a Christ most just,
  And so like souls in him do trust.

Then like as Christ above doth reign
In heaven high, our Saviour best;
So like with him shall be our gain,
In peace and joy and endless rest,
  If we ourselves like him do frame
  In fear of his most holy name.

To him be praise that grace doth give,
Whereby he fashioneth us anew,
And makes us holily to live
Like to himself, in faith most true;
  Which our redemption sure hath wrought,
  Like him to be most dearly bought.

FINIS

NOTES

MANKIND

12. *lavatory*. Cleansing from sin (literally, the priest's washing his hands during mass).

14. *remotion*. Inclination.   16. *participable*. Entitled to share in.

29. Perhaps refers to an audience from various social classes (T. W. Craik, *The Tudor Interlude*, p. 20). However, they are called simply 'sovereigns' many times (e.g., 25) and are referred to (334) as 'all the yemandry' (company, yeomanry).

30. *Prick*. Place.

32. Cf. 1 Cor. 12, referring to the mystical body of Christ as the Church (E). (Unless otherwise specified, Biblical references are to the Authorized Version.)

37. *food*. The eucharist.   42. *sickerly*. Certainly.   *strait*. Strict.

43. Cf. Luke 3:17 (E).

45. *calc'ation*. Probably a contraction of 'calculation' rather than 'calcation' (trampling) first recorded in 1656 in *OED*.

47. Cf. Tilley, H 245, 'Mickle head little wit' (E).   *predication*. preaching.

49. *draff*. Chaff, husks.

51. *raff*. Punning on 'Ralph' (normally spelt 'Rafe') and 'raff' (refuse).

52. Mischief mocks, 'Open your locked mouth and say a halfpennyworth'.

54. *winter corn-thresher*. If Coogan is correct that the play is assignable to Shrovetide (spring), then Mischief shows his idleness here—he will not be employed until late autumn or early winter following (cf. 547).

60. *et reliqua*. And the rest. The phrase followed the Gospel at Matins, and Coogan suggests that mockery is intended.

63. *&c*. Most probably an encouragement to improvise dialogue.

64. *Avoid*. Leave, or as Mischief misunderstands, 'dismount from a horse' —hence the sudden reference to riding.

70. *Deul*. A monosyllabic early form of 'Devil'.   72. *trace*. Dance measure.

73. *baleis*. A rod or scourge, which reappears at 812 in the hands of Mercy. New Guise asks Nowadays to make Naught dance, perhaps by striking at his feet with the baleis. Mischief probably has left the stage—he has no further speaking part until 414.

76. *wight*. Agile.   80. *shrewd*. Sharp-tongued.   82. *rule*. Disturbance.

83. *good Adam*. Good old man.   89. *scuttling*. Escaping (from the baleis).

97. *tell*. Say.   102. *set*. Phrased.

103. *new guise...new jet*. New fashion (E).

106. *simple*. Simple-minded; ignorant and hence prone to sin.

109. *like*. Perhaps 'taste' (E) or more probably ironic—i.e., 'like it or lump it'.

113. *trippet*. Tripping up.   116. Mercy's oath indicates extreme anger.

122. *and my*. E emends to 'by': however, repetition of 'name' in the synonymous 'denomination' leads to the vices' attack on Mercy's speech-style.

127. *Pravo te*. Probably 'shrew thee' (E).

134. *clerical*. Learned.   142. *Osculare fundamentum*. Kiss my behind.

143. *belly-met*. 'To the measure of the belly' (E), possibly punning on 'by limit', a term applied to ecclesiastical pardons (Coogan).

153. *demonical friary*. Alludes satirically to the Dominicans, or Black Friars, and perhaps identifies Mercy as a friar (Coogan).

154–5. Probably proverbial (E).

156. Cf. 'when the devil is blind', a proverbial expression.

159–60. Proverbial; Tilley, D 556 and G 81 (E). John Heywood, *Dialogue of Proverbs*, Part I, xi, 166–8, similarly uses these two proverbs for contemptuous dismissal.

162. s.d. 'They go out together. Let them sing.'   177. Cf. Rom. 14:12.

180. Proverbial; Cf. Gal.. 6:7 (E).   192. *perversionate*. perverted.

200. Proverbial; Tilley S 573.   202. *sustance*. Substance.

208. *bote*. Help.   211. *querelous*. Quarrelsome.   219. *hend*. Welcome.

228. Job 7:1. 'The life of man upon earth is a warfare' (Douay).

232. *adjutory*. Helper.

234. *a cherry time*. A brief time (like the cherry season).

237. *Measure is treasure*. Tilley, M 805.

241ff. Parallels in other Middle English devotional literature have been uncovered by Smart and Coogan. In *The Trial of Treasure* (1567) Inclination is bridled, and behaves like a horse.

245. *faitour*. Liar.

248. *piss my peson*. A scatological jest—a 'peson' was a staff with balls attached, used for weighing.

249. *to-ban*. Curse thoroughly; 'to' is intensive, as is 'for' (269).

252. *gesoun*. Perhaps 'scarce' (E), or if ironic, perhaps *MED*'s 'a treasure' (from gersume) or 'healthy' (from gesund).

261. *The...lever*. Tilley, S 641 (the sooner the better).

267. *daint*. Fondness.   272. *worts*. Malt, used in brewing.

274. *sithen*. Continuously. *tapster of Bury*. Could refer to a woman, hence suggesting a prostitute. Bury is Bury St Edmunds, Suffolk.

286–8. Cf. Job 23:10.

292–3. Job 1:21: 'The Lord gave, and the Lord hath taken away. As it hath pleased the Lord so it is done. Blessed be the name of the Lord' (Douay).

296. *Nice*. Wanton, lascivious.   298. *intromit*. Introduce.

302. *Titivillus*. Perhaps from 'totius vilius' (totally vile); generally regarded as a minor Devil whose task was to gather scraps of bad Latin at carelessly said church services.

304. *round*. Whisper. *cast a net before your eye*. Cf. Proverbs 12:12: 'The wicked desireth the net of evil men, but the root of the righteous yieldeth fruit.' A 'net' is a 'moral or mental entanglement' (*OED*), perhaps symbolized later by a prop carried by Titivillus.

307. *bridle*. i.e., the noose.   314. *superate*. Overcome.

315. *the...came*. That I came when I did.

316. *title*. Write down.   317. *promition*. Promise.

320. *remos*. A form of 'remotion' (cf. 14n.).

322. Job 34:15: 'Remember, man, that thou art ashes and shall return into ashes' (Douay). Line 319 is ironic.

323. *badge of mine arms*. As 'Christ's own knight' (229) Mankind would wear the Cross (Smart). 322 is Mankind's motto, which completes his coat of arms.

166

324. *feris*. Fires (rhymes with 'perverteris').

325. Psalm 18:26: 'With the pure thou wilt show thyself pure, and with the froward thou wilt show thyself froward.'

326-7. *Ecce...Jocundum/Habitare...unum*. Psalm 133:1; 'Behold how good and how pleasant it is for brethren to dwell together in unity.'

328. *mell*. Mix.   329. *delf*. Dig.   331. *fusion*. Foison, plentiful crop.

333. *Christmas song*. Christmas was a time when ribald songs were common, and the devout were warned against them (E). It may be, as well, that the vices call it a Christmas song to encourage participation by putting the audience off guard.

344. *Holike*. Punning on 'holy like' and 'hole lick'.

349. *with breding*. In haste.   370. *shrewd*. Severe, ascetic.

375. *compass*. A corruption of 'compost' (E).

382. *jewels*. i.e., testicles.

388. *leasing*. Falsehood.   391. *Cock's*. God's.

395. *subsidy*. Assistance.

398. I Samuel 17:47: 'The Lord saveth not with sword and spear.'

406. *convict*. Vanquish.   425. *Clamant*. They cry out.

426. *borrow*. Deliverance from danger.

427. *ven*. Come (imperative) (E); possibly corruption of French 'viens' or Latin 'veni'.

429. *greet*. Weep.

431. *ba*. Kiss (usually used in addressing children).

433ff. Cf. the bringing to life accomplished by the doctor in the mumming plays (Smart).

434. *Seely*. Miserable, pitiable (E).   438. *shrewd*. Dangerous, hurtful.

444. *one and one*. One by one.   447. *recumbentibus*. Knock-down blow (*OED*).

450. *interlection*. E's 'consultation' is unlikely, as no further consultation follows. Mischief's allusion to a minstrel suggests that he takes the word (elsewhere unrecorded) to mean 'interlocution'—alternating intonation of verses of Psalm, etc. Some little song routine, perhaps parodying Psalmody, would appropriately introduce Titivillus.

453. *Walsingham whistle*. No topicality has been yet uncovered. Perhaps ironic, if Naught produced a gaudy or cheap whistle which Mischief took to be a flute.

457. '*si dedero*'. 'If I give, I expect money in return', a popular expression (E).

460. *ghostly*. Devoutly.

463. *keep your tale*. Perhaps 'keep account of your money' (E); but more likely Nowadays interrupts with 'don't tell them too much'.

465. A groat was worth fourpence, and a 'pence of two pence' was a coin worth twopence.

466. *red rials*. The rose noble, worth 50p (10s) first coined in 1465 (Smart).

467. *Ye...tother*. If you can't pay one pay the other.

468. *goodman of this house*. Possibly the 'hostler' (737), or perhaps the owner of the house or inn where the play was being performed.

472. *estis vos pecuniatus?* Have you got your money?

476. *Ego sum dominancium dominus*. I am lord of lords. Cf. Deut. 10:17 and Rev. 19:16.

477. *caveatis*. Beware.

478. *trice*. Haul, snatch.   s.d. *Loquitur ad*. Speaks to.

479. *Ego probo sic.* Thus I prove it. Cf. 302n.

484. *The...whit.* 'The devil have the profits' (if I am lying); a popular expression.

488. *Non...nobis.* Not unto us, O Lord, not unto us. Cf. Psalm 115:1.

489–90. Tilley, D 233 and B 391.

494. *anon...sought.* Let it be searched speedily.

498. *the five vowels.* Probably referring to his cries of pain (a, e, i, o, u) (E).

499. *scitica.* Sciatica (usually a pain in the nerves of the hip and leg).

506–16. Sawston, Hauxton, and Trumpington are south of Cambridge, while Fullbourn, Bottisham, and Swaffham are east of it. East Walton, Gayton, Massingham, and another Swaffham are east of Lynn, Norfolk. Except for Bollman and Patrick, the intended victims are all traceable to the towns. Wood and Alington were justices, and Hammond of Swaffham was probably William Hammond, a man of importance; hence the vices will avoid them. Smart suggests that the players may have travelled by water between Cambridge and Lynn with *Mankind.*

513. *noli me tangere.* Touch me not. Christ's words in the garden after the Resurrection (John 20:17); hence proverbial (Tilley, N 202).

517. *in...queck.* Hanging. The prayer by the dying in imitation of Christ (Luke 13:46) would quickly be followed by choking—which 'queck' well imitates (Coogan).

521. *neck-verse.* A Latin verse, usually from Psalm 51, which a felon would recite correctly to escape hanging for a first offence. Later, at 835, Mercy exhorts Mankind to recite this after Mankind has narrowly escaped hanging.

523. *left hand.* Associated with the Devil (cf. Matt. 24:41); clergy always bless with the right hand.

525. *avantage.* Loot.   532. *have his foot-met.* 'Take his measure' (E).

536. *By...assayed.* By the time he has finished trying.

538. *drawk...darnel.* Weeds which grow among corn; darnel looks like corn until ripe. A probable parallel is Christ's parable of the tares sown among wheat by the Devil (Matt. 13:25–41)—the tares being 'things which offend and them which do iniquity'. In the Wycliff English New Testament (1382) the translation is 'dernil', whereas in the later (Purvey) version 'tares' is used. In the play, Titivillus mixes darnel with Mankind's seed-grain as a means o ɟ sowing iniquity in his soul.

542. *send us of his sand.* Send us his message, send us his grace.

544. *overdilew.* Dig.

545. *In...Sancti.* In the name of the Father, and the Son, and the Holy Ghost (said while making the sign of the cross).

547. *at winter.* Mankind puts off sowing until late autumn, deciding to allow his fields to lie fallow. Soon 'winter' becomes 'for ever' (550).

548. *lost.* Ruined; mingled with darnel. Mankind exaggerates here because he is too lazy to winnow and purify his seed.

551. *put...dever.* Feel obliged.

552–3. Mankind's purpose to hear (i.e., say) his evensong in the fields reflects a Lollard belief that prayers are equally efficacious, wherever said (E).

555. Our Father, who art in Heaven.

556. *no...heels.* Tilley, L 136.   558. *tittle.* Whisper.

559. 'Since a short prayer pierces Heaven, cease praying.' Smart gives several parallels for the usual meaning, 'even a short prayer will reach Heaven'.

561. *avent thee.* Evacuate, defecate. Cf. 563.

570–2. Titivillus alludes to his abilities as a trickster in general, giving us one 'pretty' lesson in counterfeiting. 'Powder of Paris' is probably Paris Green which would whiten brass, making it pass for silver at dusk (Smart). Titivillus alludes to France, probably satirically (cf. 598).

579. *ad omnia quaere.* 'With a reason for everything' (E).

593. *sad.* Sound.   594. *The...dead.* Tilley, D 244.

605. *brethel.* Probably a variant of 'brothel'. As a noun it means 'frequenter of a bawdy house' (709); hence probably 'abandon' or 'cuckold' as a verb here. *leman.* Mistress, whore.

608. *avows.* Ellipsis of 'I make a vow'.

612. *smattering.* Probably 'painted' (cf. besmotered).

613–38. Separate entrances are supplied, since the vices left in different directions and begin here by telling each other their experiences.

615. *Saint Patrick's way.* Purgatory.

620. *conned.* Either 'conde' or 'coude' in the ms. The sense seems to be 'recited'. Having recited his neck-verse, Mischief has escaped hanging and is a convict, but at 622 his imminent execution is referred to. Later (643) he does not mention a capital sentence. Probably this minor confusion would not be noticed in performance.

622. *lighly.* i.e., 'likely' (handsome) (E).

629. *Saint Audrey's holy bend.* A silk scarf, hallowed to give aid for neck ailments at the shrine of St Audrey in Ely Cathedral (E).

630. *dishes.* Disease.   631. *running ringworm.* Alluding to the welt on his neck.

642. *scoured.* Worn down, polished with wearing (E).

645. *halsed.* Embraced.   648. *doubler.* A platter or large plate.

650. *chesance.* Way of getting money (E).

661. *As...heaven.* Tilley, G 175 (a surprising oath for Nowadays!).

667. *sub forma juris.* i.e., 'in forma juris'–'in legal manner'. *dasard.* Dullard.

669. *come or sen.* Tenants had to attend the manorial court or send acceptable excuses (E).

672–3. *tolled...told.* The ms. reads 'tolde' twice, but a quibble is likely between taking part of Mankind's gown as a toll or fee, and thereby being able to 'tell' or count out the profits (E).

684. *running fist.* Cursive handwriting.

687. *it...hand.* 'It would behoove you' (E); 'if you know what's good for you'.

688–91. Naught's incorrect macaronics parody the usual introduction to a court record. 'Carici' should be 'Curia', 'regitalis' should be 'regis', and 'nullateni' is an error for 'nullatenus' (E). With these corrections: 'A general court held/In a place there good ale is/In the year of the reign of King/Edward by no means.' The last line, Smart suggests, dates the play between October 1470 and April 1471, when Edward IV had been temporarily deposed.

692. Continuing the nonsense, Naught places the court date at 'yesterday in February'. The second half of the line probably means 'the year is entirely wanting' (Smart).

693. *Tully.* 'Cicero', mocking Naught's scholarship, rather than his legal abilities. E suggests 'writer of Latin'.

698. *feat tail.* Well-fitted jacket (with tails, or flaps?).

704. *good fellows.* Disreputable louts (cf. French *bonhomme*). As 705 shows,

the vices have nothing to do with 'the goodman' (a common term for a farmer).

715. *Mass...Prime*. A confused list of the church's services. The 'hours' were the seven occasions of obligatory daily prayer, one of which was 'Prime'.

718. *da pacem*. 'Give peace' (a sword or dagger) (E).

734. *Stow, statt, stow!* Ho woman, ho! 'Stow' was a hunting call (E).

737. *football*. Football was frowned upon, as it was then like a street-riot, not an organized game.

744. *caren*. Carrion. *odible*. Odious.

747. *apprehensible*. Unrecorded by *OED*; 'able to perceive how' (E).

749. *passible*. Liable to suffer (discharging man's liability).

752. *dispectuous*. Contemptible.   754. *fane*. Obsolete word, for 'vane'.

755. *In...treason*. Tilley, T 549.

756. *perversiose*. Perverse.   757. *despectible*. Despicable.

759–60. The 'versifier' is unidentified, but as Smart notes Gower's *Confessio Amantis*, Bk. V, 4917 ff., parallels the idea. In translation, 'Christ's law, the law of nature, and all human laws condemn the ungrateful man and mourn his birth.'

764. *unparty*. Aside.   767. *allectuous*. Alluring (E). Not in *OED*.

772. Eccl. 1:2.

776. *predilect*. Preferred to all others.   *ubi es?* Where are you?

776–7. The staging is unclear to 810. Mercy must leave to seek Mankind, and he encounters the vices who jeer after him. The vices seemingly enter one at a time, and are all present by 792 for the parliament (by which time Mercy is out of earshot).

777. *prepotent*. All-powerful (meant ironically).

778. *lesse*. i.e., 'lease' (falsehood), preserved for rhyme.   780. *hic*. Here.

781. *creek*. A secret corner or nook (*OED*). Mankind apparently is attempting to hide.

784. *domine domine dominus*. Lord of lord of lords.

785. *cape corpus*. Writ of arrest (E).

786. *non est inventus*. A sheriff's deposition that a fugitive has not been found (E). Nowadays is confusing Mercy (probably purposely) since such a return would *follow* the issue of a cape corpus.

787. *My...shot*. Tilley, B 512. Naught uses the expression literally (788) to refer to himself evacuating (probably offstage).

790. *tackles*. Arrows (or, as Naught implies, turds).

793. *belive*. At once.

800. *whip...coat*. 'Keep it under your hat'.   801. *shon*. Shoes.

814. *copped*. Perhaps 'heaped up' (E); or punning on 'coped' (i.e., wearing a cope or vestment during a solemn execration or commination). *Saint Davy*. Perhaps St David, renowed for asceticism.

819. *solacious*. Consoling.   820. *criminous*. Guilty.

826. *iterate*. Repeated.   830. *reduce*. Recall.

831. Cf. Psalm 77:10 and Proverb 12:7: 'For I will remember the years of the right hand of the most high; the wicked are overthrown and are not.'

835. '*Miserere mei, Deus.*' 'Be merciful unto me, O God.' Cf. 521n.

838. *precise*. Make clear.

839. *Nolo...inquit*. Ezekiel 33:11 is fairly close (E): 'He does not seek after the death of a sinner'.

843. The proverb is elsewhere unrecorded.

844. *privy unto.* Knowledgeable in the secrets of.

848. *deambulatory.* Cloister or covered walk.

850. Cf. Ecclus. 5:4–7 (Douay). *notary.* Notable.

855. Cf. John 8:11 (translated in 857).

856. *avowtry.* Adultery. 862–3. Perhaps proverbial (Smart).

867. *usque...quadrantem.* 'Even to the uttermost farthing'. Cf. Matt. 5:26 (E).

871. 2 Cor. 6:2: 'Behold, now is the accepted time; behold, now is the day of salvation.'

873. *premiable.* Deserving of reward.

876. *suavious.* Pleasing. *recreatory.* Source of comfort.

879. *compatient.* Sympathetic. 880. *swimmeth.* Overcomes with grief.

885. *brunt.* Assault, temptation.

887. *Jacula...ledunt.* Literally, 'exposed darts harm the less', i.e., known evils are avoidable. The proverb is unrecorded in English.

889. *the Flesh and the Fell.* A common tautology, 'the flesh and the skin', meaning our physical nature.

899. *Libere...nolle.* Freely assent, freely refuse.

904. *here then.* Before (E).

906–7. The Lord keep you from all evil/In the name of the Father, the Son, and the Holy Ghost. Line 906 is from Psalm 121:7.

909. *favoural patrociny.* Favourable protection.

916. *prove.* Experience. 918. *playferes.* Companions.

A PLAY OF LOVE

3. *as.* As if. 7. *port.* Social position or deportment.

16. i.e., 'all this is, in the way it happens, unknown to me' (ellipsis of 'is').

33. *in ure.* In practice.

39. *as who saith rightly.* 'As the saying goes'.

43. *supposed.* Alleged, told.

52–7. Puns upon 'time'. Line 52 means 'No time is the right time to present my suit to ease my woe'; 54, 'Time always chooses the wrong time [to present] my worthiness'; 55–6, 'Time presents no time at which I can hope of any grace, in any time or place'; 57, 'Therefore until time has brought my time so far towards its end'.

68–9. *incontinently...see.* 'That you will see immediately'.

75. *pretend.* Attempt. 76. *circumstance.* Inessential arguments.

79. *of...nothing.* 'By one whom I love not at all'.

95. *or.* Before. 105. *in manner.* Habitually.

129–33. Beheading was reserved for persons of rank, and customarily the executioner begged their pardon.

141. *for shorter end.* To be brief. *put case.* Suppose.

146. *affection.* Partiality or bias.

180. *to...skill.* 'As those able to understand will realize'.

186. *as.* Namely, for example. 194. *disease.* Discomfort.

203. *Doubt.* Fear.

208. *principal.* Primary argument, major premise (cf. 148).

212. *seld.* Infrequent. 237. *indifferent.* Impartial.

245–6. s.d. *with a song.* Not given; Lover-loved (1372) refers to the lines that follow as 'my saying at my first entry'.

255. Ellipsis of 'we' before 'proceed'.

262. *like...pretended.* 'Similar outward signs always are indicated'.

264. *speed.* Success.

270-3. i.e., the sufferer may sooner conceal a raging fever than he can hide the least of all the thousand pains stemming from love.

278. *rebound.* Reverberation, echo.

303. *rudeness or lewdness.* Lack of manners or ignorance.

306. *losel.* Idle fellow, rascal.

323. *as...woodcock.* Tilley, W 746 (woodcocks were proverbially foolish).

325. *use.* Deal with [me].   348. *purpose.* Argument.

350. *at one point.* Of a settled opinion.

351. *smirkest.* Neatest.   359. *curstest.* Most shrewish.

394. *scorneth.* Degrades.

399. *nobs.* A contemptuous endearment, such as 'sweetheart'.

400. *a...ye.* i.e., 'good luck'.

405. *daw.* Jackdaw (a symbol of foolishness, like the woodcock).

406. *force.* Care.

410. *mumming.* Acting in dumb-show. No-lover-nor-loved means that he needs not prepare for the coming argument.

429-68. These two-stress iambic lines (printed as two columns in *Q*) recall the 'Skeltonics' of such poems as Skelton's 'The tunnying of Elynour Rummyng' —which begins with a satiric description of a 'comely gyll [girl]/That dwelt on a hyll'. Heywood is perhaps imitating Skelton's tumbling catalogue for humorous effect: 'Droupy and drowsy,/Scurvy and lowsy;/Her face all bowsy,/Comely crynklyd,/Woundersly wrynklyd...'.

448. *gossips.* Companions.

451. *whole.* F reads 'hole', and in view of the next item described (457) a pun is likely.

459. *mickle.* Large.

469. *Saint Catherine's wheel.* St Catherine was tortured upon a wheel and beheaded in Alexandria (c. A.D. 307): hence her emblem was a spiked wheel.

470. *round...heel.* A bawdy allusion; round heels having no 'hold' to them (472) supposedly allowed a woman to fall backwards more easily, and hence denoted promiscuity.

475. *pastance.* Pastime.

486. *dissimuling.* An aphetic derivative of 'dissimulating'.

488. *nock.* End, limit (literally, the notch at the end of an arrow).

489. *triced her.* Tripped her up; gave her a fall.

515. *point device.* Properly dressed.   516. *trull.* Loose woman, trollop.

525. *in rate.* In estimation (cf. 563).

530. *form.* A type of bench without a back.

570. *worth...shoe.* Cf. Tilley, S 382: 'Not worth shoe buckles'.

572. *moccum moccabitur.* Tilley, M 1031: 'He who mocks shall be mocked'.

586. *brother.* Companion, fellow.   595. *weight.* Suffering, grief.

598. *set...eye.* Wept.

605-6. *like...back.* Cf. Tilley, B 724: 'To stick like burrs'.

608. *disguising.* A masque-like entertainment involving speeches and dancing by disguised revellers; hence 'pastime'.

613. *ought.* Owed.

621. *Mother.* A common address to elderly women of the lower classes.

634. *B.* Perhaps for 'bawd'?

647. *jet.* Swagger, brag. 648. *jetted.* Moved jerkily.

662. *nosegay.* A small bunch of flowers carried near the nose to ward off bad smells; hence, 'something to be kept in mind'.

680. *it drinketh bittersweet.* i.e., it is pleasant tasting but has (like worm medicine) unpleasant effects.

682. *worm.* A whim (cf. also 680).

683. *this medicine.* i.e., jealousy and dread.

686. *not...onion.* Tilley, O 66.

693. *he...find.* Tilley, S 213 from Matt. 7:8. Cf. *Lusty Juventus,* 164.

702. *this great mist.* i.e., your dimness of sight.

703. *coot.* Another foolish bird. Cf. Skelton's *Philip Sparowe,* 408: 'And also the mad coote,/With a balde face to toote'.

706. A bawdy allusion. Cf. Tourneur's *Revenger's Tragedy:* 'May be his groom/ O'th'stable begot me; you know I know not./He could ride a horse well' (I.ii.135).

710–13. As No-lover-nor-loved puns on 'before' referring to time and place, he must quickly leap around Loved-not-loving.

721–2. Cf. Tilley, F 1: 'the face is the index of the heart'.

738. *grated.* Querulously argued.

758. *that cometh acrook.* A bawdy quibble on 'dishonestly', and 'crookedly' (depending upon the sexual sense of 'take', and 'do' in 760).

760. Cf. *Lusty Juventus,* 272–3n.

771. *case.* Situation, perhaps with a bawdy quibble alluding to the female sexual organs (Partridge, *Shakespeare's Bawdy,* p. 76).

775. *wood.* Mad.

783–93. Puns on various senses of 'join' and its derivatives. In 783, 785, 787, 788, 790, and 791 the sense is 'ally' or 'associate'. A joiner is a cabinetmaker who, in partnership with the Vice, would connect the characters as closely as the joints in woodwork. Cf. *As You Like It,* III.iii.73ff.: 'this fellow will but join [marry] you together as they join wainscot'.

794. *in fleeces.* Like tufts of sheeps' wool. 795. *departed.* Separated.

796. *partlike.* Proportionally. 805. *noddy.* Fool.

811. *God's forbod.* God forbid. 813. *common case.* Case at common law.

815. *serjeant.* Serjeants-at-law were barristers from among whom Common Law judges used to be chosen.

817–19. Alluding to the 'reverence' due to a judge in court and to a mock curtsy by Loved-not-loving, who receives a salutation ('beck') in return.

820. *Saint Antony.* Perhaps Antony of Padua (patron saint of pregnant women) who suddenly revealed learning and eloquence beyond the scope of his formal training (as the Vice presently fancies is his case).

835. *pith.* Main argument. 838. *other.* Either.

845. *lever.* Rather.

846. *ride.* Probably with a bawdy connotation (cf. 706n.).

847. *paternoster while.* A brief while—time for one 'Pater Noster' (Lord's Prayer). Tilley, P 99.

848. *define.* Distinguish, discover.

850. 'Maids say nay, and take it' (Tilley, M 34) has a bawdy application, 'your pain' being the physical discomfort of such a union. In 852 'her pain' of forsaking is the emotional distress involved in a lost opportunity.

872. *gastfull.* Dreadful, ghastly. *uneath.* Scarcely, with difficulty.

873. *for mine ears.* i.e., to relieve them from hearing the suit.

886. *only.* Alone. 900. *delightful.* Delighted.

910. *endure.* Continue. 916. *extinct.* Extinguish.

920. *your own salve your own sore.* The will, which could heal (salve) his pain by ending love, is a sore (in that it began loving and continues to do so).

924. *hove.* Linger. 930. *sow.* Ingot.

936. *minion.* An affectionate nickname for a woman.

937. *demurrer in law.* A pleading which admits the facts of the opponent's case, but denies that he is entitled to relief or damages (cf. 921–30). In a generalized sense, 'impasse' or 'deadlock'.

944. *for your part.* i.e., of Loved-not-loving's case.

955. *dell.* i.e., 'deal', part.

972. *let.* Hindrance. 986. *seld when.* Seldom.

991. *worth...fly.* Cf. Tilley, F 396: 'Not worth a fly'.

993. *laid...water.* Laid aside (Tilley, W 108).

1022–3. Lover-not-loved claims that because of imbalance of the four humours he suffers from an excess of all at once. Cf. 1183–1222 for the Vice's parody.

1032. *by attorney.* i.e., through the agency of the Vice's hand, which carries the heat of the posteriors up to meet the cold of Lover-not-loved's nose. This may explain why Lover-not-loved's lips smack (1034–5)—an action which the Vice takes as an invitation for him to repeat his action, carrying 'more moisture'. The hapless victim apparently forgoes breathing, understandably (1036).

1036. *quicker.* More lively.

1052. *Gib's feast.* 'Gib' was a name often applied to cats (especially tom cats) and to old crones or hags; hence perhaps the kiss would be like kissing 'something the cat dragged in', or an old ugly hag.

1070. *in fine.* To make an end. 1077. *frustrate.* Idle; beside the point.

1087–8. *upper end...nether end.* Some action placing Loved-not-loving and Lover-not-loved facing the audience is called for, since they are now to act as judges. The Vice makes a bawdy quibble on 'nether end'.

1115. *secondly.* Cf. 'second imagination' (1117)—'second-rate'.

1137. 'Are not at all the sort of thing that concerns me in any way.'

1156. *feeling.* Deeply felt, vivid. 1164. *twink.* Wink.

1174–5. 'This head utterly abhors that these eyes should wink longer than love occupies this heart in thought.' The reference to dreams (1176) clarifies—sleep is despised unless it brings dreams of the sweetheart.

1179. Cf. the common oath, 'Christ's cross be my speed' (aid).

1184. *this man's case.* Alluding to Lover-not-loved.

1191. *brought about.* Turned around or turned topsy turvy.

1194. *stint.* Cessation. 1208. *cast.* Trick.

1208–18. The Vice ridicules lovers' physical sufferings (cf. 990–1023) through ludicrous overstatement. No-lover-nor-loved argues that love is worse than Hell's torments, while supposedly being pleasurable ('by any pleasant mind'). He blasphemously suggests that God made a mistake in not associating love with Lucifer, rather than God and Heaven. Line 1217 is obscure, but the sense probably is 'if anything evil is to come to Lucifer, it will have to be love'—God has corrected His mistake, and love is now the only evil in the world.

1218. *love...blood.* Love shall cause the suffering or letting of blood.

1222. *the black jaundice.* A virulent form of the disease then commonly associated with jealousy (which the Vice implies is natural to lovers).

1225. 'That confirms any proof of your case' (legal terminology).

1245. *Look...man.* Tilley, M. 838.

1263–4. 'If you allow (endure) any pleasures to yourself, then you must also feel more displeasures than you admit.'

1277. *rather...fortypence.* Probably proverbial—fortypence was common for 'a lot of money'.

1288. *a face.* Impudence.

1289–91. Punning on shame as 'disgrace' and 'the sense of having offended'.

1311–12. s.d. *coppintank.* A high sugar-loaf hat described by Sir Thomas North as 'narrow in the top, as the Kings of the Medes...do use to wear them' (*OED*).

1327. *flush.* A sudden spurt.   1328. *bush.* An ample head of hair.

1338. *rub him.* Chafe his temples or wrists (to help him recover consciousness).

1344. *speak parrot.* Tilley, P 60; i.e., speak foolishly or by rote.

1347. *jakes.* A privy (perhaps here with an outside exit to empty the waste).

1361. *matter of record.* Valid evidence (a legal term).

1365. *fact.* Action.   1372–5. Cf. 253–9.   1385. *stake.* Winnings, wager.

1392. *by my sheath.* A petty oath found also in More's *Confutation of Tyndale* (*OED*).

1406. *declaring such show.* Declaring such matters to be shows (vanities).

1436. *slick...eel.* Tilley, E 60.   1444. *meat.* Provender, food.

1451. *the ton.* The one; one of them (cf. 1541).

1453. *is for me.* Represents me; stands for me.

1466. *for partial.* Because of partiality.

1479. *stiffly.* Stubbornly.   1485. *direction.* Rule, guide.

1493. *lubber.* F's 'lober' might be a misreading for 'lover'; however cf. 513–14, where 'lober' apparently means 'lubber'.

1506. *piecing.* Piecing together, coming to understand.

1512. *your undeserved pain.* i.e., the trouble taken to decide the case.

1532. 'In these facts his case appears in its worst light.'

1542. *the rood's mother.* The Virgin Mary.   1556. *taketh.* Comes into.

1567. *Christ's precept.* Cf. *Lusty Juventus*, 272–3.

1584–5. i.e., in human love contentation may not easily be enjoyed. (All three lovers are either in pleasure rather than contentation, or in pain which denies it.)

1589. *in fine.* At the end; at death.

1592. *presenting.* Making present; setting forth.

LUSTY JUVENTUS

1. *Gen. 8.* Verse 21: 'The imagination of man's heart is evil from his youth.'

2. *Jere. 17.* Verse 9: 'The heart is deceitful above all things, and desperately wicked: who can know it?'

5. *Ecclus. 30.* At line three in *Q1*. Verses 1–15 advise on the bringing up of children, and parts of this are echoed in the following six lines.

14. Cf. Tilley, N 49: 'That which Nature gives no man can take away'.

45. *pight.* Resolved.

54. *hold them as much.* Do the same to them; make them wait as long.

55. *keep....touch.* Keep promise.

87. *appety.* Altered for rhyme; cf. 61. (*Q1* has 'appetyt').

96. *Ephesians.* 5:15–16.

104. *Deuteronomy.* 29:10–11. A free rendition is given at 107–9.

123–5. Possibly alluding to the parable of the talents; cf. 315–16n.

178. *blind their sight.* A common Biblical echo: cf. Isa. 29:18, and Matt. 11:5.

196–7. Psalm 1:1–2.

198–200. Psalm 94:12.

201. *Christ...Gospel.* Luke 11:28.

205–7. *the Galathi.* Gal. 5:22–3.

211. *Saint Paul.* Heb. 11:6.

213. Rom. 14:23.

228. Rom. 4:5: 'But to him that worketh not, but believeth on him that justifieth the ungodly, his faith is counted for righteousness.'

232. Cf. John 15:5: 'I am the vine, ye are the branches; He that abideth in me and I in him, the same bringeth forth much fruit.'

236–7. I Peter 1:18: 'Forasmuch as ye know that ye were not redeemed with corruptible things...from your vain conversation received by tradition from your fathers.' Both Geneva and the Authorized Version read 'conversation' (i.e., 'manner of living'): the plural here, doubtless intended for rhyme, does not make as good sense.

258. *intents.* Endeavours, religious practices.

263. *the wise Solomon.* Really from Psalm 111:10, not the Book of Wisdom. 'Solomon', however, supplies a rhyme. Cf. also Tilley, S 609: 'As wise as Solomon'.

267–9. Cf. Matt. 22:37–9.

272–3. Matt. 7:12 (*Q1*'s 'sixt' is a misprint).

276. *Christ's Testament.* The New Testament, which Juventus is still carrying at 616–18. One wonders which translation was given to him. If my conjectures about dating are correct (see 1153–62n.), this gift of a New Testament would be very apposite. In 1546 a royal decree prohibited the use of both the available translations of the New Testament (Coverdale's and Tyndale's), but with the accession of Edward VI this decree was reversed and new editions of both translations were printed.

280. Probably based upon the common idea of Jesus as the water of life (cf. for example John 4:13–15).

292. *conversation.* Cf. 236–7n.

316. *talent.* Alluding to the parable of the talents (Matt. 25). The slothful servant is given *one* talent, as is Juventus here (probably ironically). The gloss in the Geneva Bible sums up: 'This similitude teacheth how we ought to continue in the knowledge of God, and do good with those graces that God hathe giuen us.'

325. *this gear.* My plotting, machinations.   329. *deluded.* Frustrated.

337. *inventions.* Fictions, false doctrine.

338–48. Cf. 451–7. The Devil laments the Reformation's influence on the younger generation, in keeping with the play's idea that the attitudes of the young are more easily formed (e.g., 347–8).

349. *swage.* An aphetic derivative of 'assuage'.

351. *carnal.* Cf. Rom. 8:17. The opposition of flesh and spirit, taken literally by the dramatist, underlies the course of Juventus in the play.

176

352. *taste*. Try.

363. A farmer would be interested in the sex of stock, since sows would be more valuable for breeding.

364. *butcher*. Possibly a topical allusion to the law of 1549 decreeing abstinence from flesh during Lent and at certain other times of year. Some butchers, who were able to obtain licences to kill during Lent, became very prosperous, and abuses were common (cf. *2 Henry VI*, IV.iii.3). The trade may, however, merely identify Hypocrisy as bloodthirsty.

366. *Sancti Amen*. An oath (cf. *Mankind*, 545n.). Latin identifies adherence to Catholicism.

368. *chapman*. Peddler, merchant.   384. *flower*. The 'pick', the 'best'.

388. *Flanders pin*. Cf. Tilley, P 334: 'Not worth a pin', and F 342: 'Flanders pieces [bolts of cloth] that look fair at a distance but coarse near at hand.' Flanders was reputed as a manufactory of shoddy goods.

397. *graff*. Graft, implant.   403. *sodomitry*. Sodomy.

405. *superstition*. Belief induced by fear, ignorance.

417. *stocks...stones*. Images.

418. *clouts*. Shreds of cloth, perhaps referring to the veneration of what were thought to be fragments of Christ's shroud, or perhaps to service-cloths.

421. *rochets*. Linen vestments, like surplices, worn by bishops or abbots.

431. *sprites*. Spirits (preserved for rhyme).

432. *palm*. Probably alluding to the custom of carrying palm leaves in a Palm Sunday procession.

433. *cream*. Chrism, or holy oil.   437. *trim-trams*. Absurd practices.

481. *at the bate*. At strife, at loggerheads.   492. *iwis*. Certainly.

498 ff. Remarkably, Hypocrisy uses none of the weapons mentioned in his earlier set speech, nor does he attempt to win Juventus back to the practices mentioned. That would perhaps have involved the play in serious discussion of theology, whereas the plotting here simply implies a kinship between Roman Catholicism and loose morals.

549. *feathered*. Fledged, ready to fly from the nest.

550. *his...gathered*. Cf. Tilley, C 868 (i.e., he is well-prepared).

585. *cry...winning*. Be left behind, miss out on something.

585–6. *she...her*. Used instead of 'it', 'its', referring respectively to Juventus's plan to attend the preaching, and his religiosity in general.

592. *spurt*. A brief frolic.   602. *and*. If (with omission of 'he').

610. *Doctor*. Ironically, Juventus has mocked 'Doctors divine' earlier (101).

616. *portas*. A small breviary. *OED* quotes Act 3 & 4 Edward VI c. 10: 'All Bookes called Manuelles Legends Pyes Portuyses Prymars...shalbe... abolished'. Juventus takes it as an insult to call the New Testament by a name with Catholic associations (617). Cf. 276n.

625. *to...burn*. To have been burned at the stake. The Catholic Church frowned upon Bible-reading by the laity and set tradition and authority above the Scriptures. Cf. 633–6.

628. *halter...cord*. Hypocrisy slyly evades Juventus's question by calling names—'You're fit only for hanging or burning' (punishments for, respectively, treason and heresy).

655. *gear*. Nonsensical talk.   657. *ruth*. Sorrow, calamity.

666. *pass*. Care.   680. *do...lust*. Follow your own pleasures.

681. *affinity*. Companions.

682. *beam...eye.* Cf. Matt. 7:3–5. The Geneva gloss makes clear the teaching about hypocrisy: 'for hypocrites hide their owne fautes, and seke not to amende them, but are curious to reproue other mens'.

685. *joining...plough.* Country people, rude bumpkins.

692–3. *beat...flush.* Beating flushes game for hunters. Hypocrisy means that he can drive all before him.

698. *the pie feast.* It is impossible to trace this reference, especially since Hypocrisy only takes his victim to breakfast in a kitchen, where they are entertained by a servant-girl in the absence of the master and mistress of the house (cf. 760, 787). It could be a slang term, like 'nosh-up', or else simply a promise of what will be for breakfast, connnoting gluttony. Cf. 707–9.

701. *a furney card.* 'Furney' is recorded only as a verb in *OED*, meaning 'to procure'. It is probably a marked or false card, giving the player an advantage (cf. the modern 'trump card'), and the line likely means 'I've got a trick or ploy up my sleeve' (i.e., Abominable Living). The gaming terminology is echoed in Juventus's later entry (935 ff.) dicing.

707–8. Cf. Tilley, P 621: 'Better some of a pudding than none of a pie'. Perhaps this suggested the use of 'pie feast', or cf. next note.

710. As Nosworthy points out, this line is paralleled in the third of seven Lenten sermons preached in 1549 by Latimer. In both instances, the phrase is a response to a speaker who treats a pudding as a small meal, and it indicates an inordinate love of food.

712–13. This 'shift' is to be a 'follower'—one who lurks about the servants in great houses, hoping to befriend one to feed and support him.

729. *mary.* Marrow. Perhaps proverbial, but unrecorded in Tilley.

732. *a man...making.* Cf. Tilley, M 162: 'A man of God's making' (i.e., 'just the sort of man we need').

767. *The...go.* Tilley, G 468: 'To worship the ground another treads on'.

800. *in your smock.* In your petticoat, half undressed. Juventus is being very daring, albeit perhaps somewhat adolescent.

805. *eat...good.* Tilley, M 846: 'A hungry man is an angry man'—dinner will calm Juventus down.

811. *prove.* Try.

816. *men's flesh.* Women, known as 'man's meat' (Tilley, M 490).

822. *smick-smack.* Frequent kissing.

823. *tick-tack.* 'Touch and take' (*OED*)—an old variety of backgammon using a board with holes on the edges into which pegs were placed for scoring. The bawdy quibble is obvious.

827. *smock smell.* Cf. 800n.: 'promiscuity' is perhaps closest.

828. *set...tune.* Perhaps meant generally, but perhaps alluding to venereal disease, one result of which was the appearance of sores or carbuncles on the nose which might lead to its eventual removal.

835. *this...sleight.* There's trickery here.

836. *out of conceit.* Out of [her] estimation.

853. *I wos.* i.e., I wot (I know). *it...twice.* i.e., you should have thought twice before saying that.

857. *cheeks.* Sides.

862. *crouching...owl.* i.e., be afraid to show my face.

870. *lay...flesh.* Belabour with blows. 872. *shall.* Must.

882. *because.* In order that.

178

887. *Report.* Repeat. Perhaps each verse is to be sung twice, the second time with audience participation (as in *Mankind*).

907. *abusion.* Perversion or outrage.

902–36. Good Counsel's generalized lament is in keeping with Hypocrisy's avowed intentions (cf. above, 498n.): Juventus has not apparently fallen from Protestantism to Catholicism, but into loose living and sin generally.

938. *sins and sice.* Corruption of 'cinque and cise' (five and six), a dice game. Cf. *Like Will To Like*, 933. Interestingly, Juventus appears as a result of mis-hearing Good Counsel, just as in *Mankind*, 98, the vices claim to have appeared in response to a call from Mercy.

943. *the terrible plagues.* Possibly referring the plagues in Revelation 9:20 afflicting those who 'repented not of the works of their hands'.

945. *capernite.* OED first records this as a Scottish word in 1719, 'capernoite' (i.e., head).

951. *lose my coat.* i.e., at dice (paralleling Mankind's loss of part of his coat, as a visual symbol of degeneration). At 999 Juventus's modish fashions are mentioned—like Mankind's 'jolly jacket'.

952. *trill the bones.* Roll the dice.

953. *when...pen.* Tilley, I 75.   959. *the prophet Osey.* Hosea 4:1–2.

975. *touch...again.* Juventus has apparently threatened to strike Good Counsel, and does so here again.

987. *Saint Paul.* Cf. Rom. 13:14.

990–1. *fifth to the Galathians.* vv. 16–17 are paraphrased in these lines, on which the whole play supplies a comment.

999. *cut and jag.* Synonyms. 'Jags' were the exaggerated slashes in vogue at the time on sleeves, etc.

1000. *great...mouth.* Cf. Tilley, G 379: 'The gospel is in your mouth' (not in the heart).

1003. Heb. 10:26–7.

1008. Matt. 12:31–2 treats of blasphemy of the Holy Ghost, which the Geneva gloss sees as concerning 'he that striueth against the trueth which he knoweth, and against his owne conscience'.

1017. *laugh...scorn.* Cf. Psalm 22:8.

1046. *Ezekiel.* 1047–8 render the sense of Ezekiel 33:9.

1050. Ezekiel 18:32.

1056. The interpretation given to Heb. 10:26–7, here attributed to Augustine, was the accepted one—the Geneva gloss explains: 'That is, forsake Jesus Christ, as Iudas, Saul, Arrius, Iulian the apostat did'.

1063. *Christ himself.* John 11:25.

1075. *the prodigal son.* Luke 15:11–31. This parable underlies a number of plays of the period, such as *Misogonus, Nice Wanton,* and *The Disobedient Child.*

1084–5. Matt. 7:14–15.

1091. *What is the man.* i.e., 'Is there a man?'

1094. *wait.* Be ready.

1114. *fruits of a true Christian.* Matt. 7:20: 'By their fruits ye shall know them.' Cf. also 205, 232 above.

1128. Probably proverbial, but not in Tilley. It parallels Mercy's 'iacula prestita minus ledunt' (*Mankind*, 887).

1131–6. A striking parallel to a situation in *Everyman*, when the hero is failed at death by Friendship and Kindred.

1146. *nice.* 'Delightful' or 'wanton' (perhaps punning on the meanings).

1153–62. In the second and third quartos all the references to the king are altered to refer to the queen (except 'his' in 1162). Probably the original performance of the play occurred during the reign of Edward VI when it was highly topical. The fragmentary records make dating of the first edition very difficult: however, the play's first publisher, Abraham Vele, began printing about 1550, so it may well be that *Lusty Juventus* was printed soon after being first performed. Revisions in the reign of Elizabeth indicate revival of the play.

1158. *ca< ptain>.* A rhyme for 'thing', 'understanding', and 'reign' is needed, and Hawkins's suggestion is closer than the 'servant' of *Q2–3* (revised because of the inappropriateness of terming a woman a captain, or leader of troops). See Nosworthy, p. xx.

LIKE WILL TO LIKE

1–2. Cicero's 'Like will to like' was a common proverb (Tilley, L 286), and in the title of this play Fulwell may have originated a variation separately recorded by Tilley (L 287). Pointing to classical sources, and using other Latin tags in the play, is the parading of knowledge attacked by Nashe as 'a most vaine thing...in many universities...If of a number of shreds of [Tully's] sentences he can shape an oration, from all the world he carries it awaie, although in truth it be no more than a fooles coat of many colours' (*The Unfortunate Traveller* in *Works*, ed. McKerrow, ii, 251). It is difficult to ascertain the source of Fulwell's Latin tags, although it seems likely that various collections of proverbial and pithy sayings, such as Erasmus's *Adagia* or Taverner's *Garden of Wisdom*, supplied them.

11. *whilere.* Some time ago. Though the Prologue says he has spoken 'The name of this matter', the title does not appear in the text: probably he announced it before commencing his prologue.

32. *dump.* Low spirits (now only in the plural).

39. The non-sequitur may indicate an opportunity to improvise dialogue as the Vice 'warms up' his audience.

47. *angle.* Corner. Nichol may be referring to a feature common to the halls of the period—the 'ingle nook' near the fireplace.

59. *wings.* Lateral projections at the shoulders, like epaulettes.

60. *chitterlings.* Small intestines; hence, pleated ruffs, which looked like coiled intestines, were later called chitterlings.

59–63. The new fashions mentioned were attacked by the moralists of the period, notably Philip Stubbes in his *Anatomy of Abuses* (1583), Ch. III. Nichol Newfangle's name is associated with modish fashion. Fynes Morison observed that 'no people in the world is so curious in new fangles as they of England be' (*OED*).

63. *buskins.* Half boots. 71. *Sancte Benedicite.* 'Bless ye the holy one'.

74. *Lucifer.* Traditionally, Satan's name before his fall from heaven (cf. Isa. 14:12).

79. *apaid.* Pleased.

84. *great bears.* Indicates Lucifer's probable costume. He is 'bottle-nosed' (89): the traditionally large grotesque Devil's nose appears in masks such as those illustrated in Allardyce Nicoll, *Masks, Mimes, and Miracles*, fig. 130.

87–8. Nichol suggests that the Devil's nose be used as a tent—a surgical appliance to distend and cleanse a wound (here, Nichol's fundament).

97. *our Lady of Walsingham.* Alluding to the shrine of the Virgin at Walsingham (destroyed in 1538), Nichol implies that it was dedicated to devil-worship.

112. *skipjack.* A pretentious fop or dandy.

142. *Tom Collier.* Two other plays, *Damon and Pithias* (1567) and *Grim the Collier of Croydon* (1600), introduce the stock figure of a comic collier with malapropisms and rustic speech. The stage dialect of his lines was often used for workingmen, foreigners (cf. 451 ff.), and rustic characters, and is commonly called 'cotswold speech'.

150–3. A scatological quibble (cf. 87).

176–7. s.d. A gittern (cittern) was an instrument of the guitar type, played with a plectrum. The indefinite stage direction shows that the dramatist was not writing for a particular company, and that the copy-text for *Q1* was not a theatrical prompt-copy. The direction probably means that with an instrument the song should follow the dance; while without an instrument the players should resort to the less happy arrangement of singing while dancing.

222. *buttocks made buttons.* Tilley, A 381.

227. *Joan...snout.* 'Joan' was a common term for a countrywoman (cf. 213, 569). Nichol also singles out a woman in the audience at 1183, as 'little Meg'.

229. *gooding.* Begging. The phrase is probably proverbial. Nichol may refer, however, to Tom's feather, saying 'it must be a ruffian, since he looks like a goose running around with that feather'.

241. *Similis...quaerit.* The Latin tag from *De Amicitia* which supplies the opening lines of the prologue.

246. *as...mouth.* Tilley, P 260.

259. *mountains...meet.* Tilley, M 748.

273. *in pudding time.* Tilley, P 634 (i.e., in good time, on time).

276. Tom and Tib are the jack and ace of trumps in the game of Gleek; hence the expression could mean 'as women for card games'. Alternatively, a 'tib' was a loose woman, and 'Kit' was another nickname for Katherine, so the line could be taken to allude to matching together men and loose women.

277. *Rafe.* Cf. *Mankind*, 51n., and Udall's *Ralph Roister Doister*. To 'roister' is to revel, swagger, boast, etc.

299. Proverbial, recalling Mark 10:25: 'It is easier for a camel to go through the eye of a needle, than for a rich man to enter into the kingdom of God'.

328. *souterly.* Resembling a shoemaker (souter); hence 'boorish'.

334. *liripup.* Part, lesson.

349. *Knave...Christmas.* Earlier (36–7) Nichol offered a knave of clubs to the audience, and this may recall that incident. It sounds like a name for some character in Christmas festivities, but it is not so recorded in Strutt's *Sports and Pastimes*.

350. *Phalaris.* A sicilian tyrant. The inventor of the bull, one Perillos, actually became its first victim at the command of Phalaris; but cf. Marlowe's *Jew of Malta*, Prologue, 23–4, which gives essentially the same version as Fulwell.

358. *Haman.* Cf. Esther 3–8. Phalaris and Haman provide parallels for the unregenerate characters in the play, whose hopes of high preferment through Nichol are similarly dashed.

361. *Harry...guard.* 'Harry' was a nickname for hangmen. The black guard was mentioned in a Lord Steward's proclamation of 1683: 'a sort of vicious,

idle, and masterless boys and rogues, commonly called the Black Guard, with divers other lewd and loose fellows' (*OED*).

367. *ere...twice*. Tilley, L 429. 380. *patrimony*. Inheritance.

382. Thomas a Waterings, on the Kent road in Surrey, and Tyburn Hill, to the west of the City of London (near the present Marble Arch), were two places of execution: hence Rafe and Tom's ignorance of them indicates their stupidity.

388. *do hold*. Is held (enjoyed or occupied as property). Cf. 911–12, where it means that Nichol's gift is part and parcel of being a beggar.

403. *their...hood*. Tilley, H 17, alluding to being threadbare because of poverty.

404. *gossips*. Friends, or possibly loose women (as Tom's reply indicates).

407. *fend their face*. Probably from both blows and cuckold's horns.

409. *shave his beard*. Reprove or harass him. Harming another man's beard was a gross insult.

410. *Flemish servants*. Cf. 448–9 below.

411. *quass*. Eat or drink excessively. While this might seem an error for 'quaff' it is the normal form here, and *OED* records three other usages.

414. *knave in grain*. A thoroughgoing knave; Tilley, K 128.

423. *bravery*. Ostentatious dress, excessive expense.

425. *pick and to steal*. A tautology; cf. the phrase 'pickers and stealers' (i.e., hands).

427. *Salisbury Plain*. A haunt of footpads and highwaymen (Sugden).

443. *Hob*. A name for a foolish rustic or clown.

448–9. *Hance*. Like Philip Fleming, Hance is an example of the Flemish servants who were boasted of earlier. The chauvinism of the period is reflected in this blunt attack. In *Wealth and Health* another Hance, characterized as a drunken Flemish shoemaker and gunner, roams England looking for work. Surprisingly, vices and virtues join in vilifying him—and this is hinted at in *Like Will*, as there seems to be no warmth in Nichol towards Hance. As 540 shows, both Philip and Hance are grotesquely fat-paunched.

450. *brinks*. Drink to; pledge.

473. Having begun some Latin toast, Hance apparently stops, noticing his empty tankard.

477. *Tu es nebulo*. 'You are a good-for-nothing'.

486. *of my guard*. Perhaps 'under my protection', or perhaps referring to the 'black guard' of 361.

487. *white son*. A favourite son.

515–17. Common proverbs: 'such...chips' (Tilley, C 94); 'such...lips' (L 326); 'like...man' (M 723); 'like...scholar' (M 724).

527. *noppy*. Heady, strong. 528. *stale*. Old, and hence strong.

547. *Domine dominus noster*. i.e., *Domini*: then the phrase would read 'lord of our lord'. Nichol's assertion that this is a part of the Paternoster (Our Father) betrays his ignorance, as does his mistaken Latin.

550. *Sanctum benedicitum*. Cf. '*sancte benedicite*' (71). Some petty oath, such as 'bless my soul' is a probable modern parallel.

573. *Snip, snap*. Probably indicates a snap of Nichol's fingers. *butter...meat*. Perhaps refers to the future poverty of Nichol's victims—cf. Tilley, M 841: 'They that have no other meat, bread and butter are glad to eat'.

575–6. Perhaps a triumphant nonsense jingle, or perhaps Nichol refers to himself as an owl (connoting wisdom) and to one (or all) of his victims as a jackanapes or fool.

595. *gear*. i.e., these doings—the word is frequently used for vice-trickery and deceptions. Cf. *Lusty Juventus*, 835n.

598–9. s.d. *counters*. Imitation coins. 601. *thrusting*. Jostling.

611. *Gib our cat*. A tom cat. Gib (a short form of Gilbert) was a common name for a male cat. Cf. *A Play of Love*, 1052n.

645. *Land...Mare*. The gallows. As at 376 ff., Nichol's trick is obvious and the foolishness of his victims remarkable.

678. *Virtutis premium honor*. Translated in the line following.

682. *so...lead*. Tilley, L 134.

684. Cf. Rom. 6:12 and 1 Peter 2:24. 693. *appose*. Interrogate, catechize.

717. *as...fire*. Proverbial; cf. Tilley, W 110: 'To mix water with fire'.

719. *dangerous*. Difficult to please.

743. *souse*. Pickled pork, especially feet and ears.

745. *as...mouse*. Tilley, M 1219. 749. *imps*. Evil rogues.

758. *Conjunctae...Honoris*. Translated in the line following.

776–7. The images are probably Biblical (cf. Rom. 16:25 and Jude 5:12).

780. *Virtus...habetur*. 'The righteous man shall possess honour and eternal life'. Fulwell uncharacteristically neither identifies nor translates his Latin tag.

820–1. *Venite...vos*. Matt. 11:28, translated in the three lines following.

895–6. *musical notation*. The harmonic and rhythmic intervals of the copy-text are preserved, but the time signature is inferred. The key was probably left to the singer. Why music should be specified here, but not for the more elaborate songs is puzzling especially in view of the rarity of music in plays of the period. Fulwell may have specified music for what appears to be a common street cry.

902. *increased...pence*. Tilley, N 194. A noble was a coin worth 33p.

904. *brought...hosen*. Tilley, P 5: explained by 921.

911. *wallet...bottle*. Cf. *Horestes*, 1042, where the Vice enters with the same props and the 'staff'—a conventional beggar's outfit.

919. *Wat*. A short form of Walter (a nickname for an auditor).

926. *banning*. Cursing. 'Curse and ban' (in the stage direction) is an intensive —cf. 'curse and swear'.

933. *cinque and cise*. Cf. *Lusty Juventus*, 938n. 935. *fain*. Forced.

941. *as...nail*. Tilley, N 4, has 'As bare as a nail'.

942. *cross...me*. Tilley, C 836—a proverb punning on the cross stamped on coins of the period.

954. *case*. Cf. 930. A pun is probable on 'situation' and 'clothes'.

991. Tilley, S 838. 1000. *Time...man*. Tilley, T 363.

1007. *stanched*. Obliterated.

1014–15. Earlier (480–7) Tom boasted of having seduced Hance from study. Perhaps he now sees the usefulness of what he earlier scoffed at, or it may be that he is making excuses for his downfall by blaming his parents.

1021. *For*. As for, as regards. 1022. *gin*. Trap.

1025. *on the score*. In debt; possibly referring to Tom's tavern reckoning or 'score'.

1036. *this wood knife*. There are a number of references to the Vices having carried wooden daggers. Feste in *Twelfth Night*, for example, says he will act as an 'old Vice' with a 'dagger of lath' (IV.ii.136). Cf. 1204–13n.

1037. *sturdy beggar.* This phrase, used to refer to masterless men who were able to work, is explained in the title of the act of 1572 (16 Elizabeth c. 5 §5) concerning 'Roges Vacaboundes and Sturdye Beggers'.

1043. *That.* In order that.

1049. *Isidorus.* Isidore of Seville (d. 636), supposed author of the Isidorian Decretals. The Latin tag is translated in line 1051.

1055. *Semper...favet.* Translated (with a change from singular to plural) in 1056–7.

1073. *confuted.* Punished.

1078–80. Indicates that Fulwell was writing for London performance—it is as a traveller from the country that Nichol's news will be of value.

1082. *the stews.* Brothels (in the suburbs of London).

1092. *throwen...perch.* Ruined; probably with the connotation of hanging.

1107. *All Hallows.* There were eight churches bearing this name in sixteenth-century London; perhaps used here for the rhyme with 'gallows'.

1131. *bower.* Husbandman (the reference to agriculture continues in the next line).

1156. *Hankin.* A nickname deriving from 'hank' (a loop of rope): 'noosing' is perhaps closest.

1157. *divide...coats.* Traditionally, the hangman received his victims' coats (cf. 1162).

1173. *leace.* Leash (preserved for rhyme).

1182. *Balaam's ass.* Num. 22:21–31: Balaam's ass refused to move because of God's intervention, thereby assisting to return Balaam to God's service.

1192. *spital.* Low-class charity hospital.

1195–6. Perhaps proverbial. Cf. Tilley, L 468: 'Better a louse (mouse) in the pot than no flesh at all'. Cf. 'a mess of souse' (743).

1202. *Ginks.* i.e., 'jinks'—the 'chinks' of metal coins.

1204–13. Samuel Harsnett, in *A Declaration of Egregious Popish Impostures* (1603), observed: 'and it was a pretty part in the old church-plays, when the nimble Vice would skip up like a jack-a-napes into the devil's neck and ride the devil a course, and belabour him with his wooden dagger, till he made him roar, whereat the people would laugh' (quoted in L. B. Cushman, *The Devil and the Vice* (Halle, 1900), p. 68). The improvisation of further business for comic effect would be likely.

1213. *Spain.* A satiric thrust, as Spain was considered Catholic and hence evil.

1222. *commodity.* Advantage.

A SONG. An optional afterpiece. Evidence for the performance of entertainments following short plays is provided by the 'Bergomask dance' performed by Bottom and his fellows (*Midsummer Night's Dream*, v.i.345).